MATURING
IN THE
CHRISTIAN LIFE

Books by Neill Q. Hamilton
Published by The Geneva Press
Maturing in the Christian Life:
A Pastor's Guide

Published by The Westminster Press
Jesus for a No-God World

Published by The Seabury Press
Recovery of the Protestant Adventure

Published by Oliver & Boyd, Ltd.
The Holy Spirit and Eschatology in Paul

MATURING
IN THE
CHRISTIAN LIFE

A PASTOR'S GUIDE

NEILL Q. HAMILTON

THE GENEVA PRESS
Philadelphia

Scripture quotations from the Revised Standard Version of the Bible are copyrighted 1946, 1952, © 1971, 1973 by the Division of Christian Education of the National Council of the Churches of Christ in the U.S.A., and are used by permission.

Book Design by Alice Derr

First edition

Published by The Geneva Press®
Philadelphia, Pennsylvania

PRINTED IN THE UNITED STATES OF AMERICA
9 8 7 6 5 4 3 2 1

Library of Congress Cataloging in Publication Data

Hamilton, Neill Quinn.
  Maturing in the Christian life.

  Includes bibliographical references.
  1. Christian life—1960–   2. Pastoral theology.
I. Title.
BV4501.2.H293   1984   253   83–20661
ISBN 0–664–24515–3 (pbk.)

To
my unpaid, mystery typist who prefers
anonymity
in this era of liberation!

I will make you fishers of people.
Mark 1:17

CONTENTS

INTRODUCTION

This book arises out of an expressed need among church leaders for guidance in the matter of faith development. Information about cognitive development (Piaget) and moral development (Kohlberg) has filtered into popular consciousness through books and periodical literature. Efforts to frame a theory of *faith* development (Fowler) upon these substructures naturally attracts more and more interest. The Discipleship and Worship Program Area of the Program Agency of The United Presbyterian Church U.S.A. has commissioned this work as a biblical-theological resource to complement the more psychological approaches to faith development.

My work with clergy in programs of continuing education had convinced me that some clearer understanding of the Christian life as a faith journey was the key to coherence and integrity in the practice of ministry today. I was just about to write my reflections on the Christian life from a New Testament point of view when the Agency and I found we had a common interest. So I have had the delightful experience of writing in continuing consultation with Program Agency staff, all under the graceful hosting of Discipleship and Worship's director, the Rev. Dr. James G. Kirk. I have prized Jim's friendship since we were in school together, but I must warn you, the reader, in all fairness to the Program Agency and its staff, that the result you are about to read is not committee production, but my own. And so I must accept sole responsibility for the end product with grateful acknowledgment for the gifts and graces so many others have contributed.

This work is primarily for clergy and as such is a labor of love. As I have surveyed the life of the church during twenty-five years of attempting to serve its needs as a theological professor, the conviction has grown in me that parish ministry is the most difficult and most crucial profession for church and world. It is most crucial because parish clergy set the tone for the life of the church. Although the ministry of the church belongs to the whole people of God, clergy and lay alike, the leadership role the institutional church assigns to the clergy makes them the pacesetters for the ministry of the whole church. It is common wisdom that little can change in the life of a congregation without the support and cooperation of its pastoral leader. The parish leader is the enabler of the ministry of the congregation.

But while the church holds the clergy responsible for the extent and quality of its ministry, it does not grant them the authority to exercise the leadership role it lays upon them. The clergy have no way to ensure that others will follow their lead. This makes pastoral ministry the most difficult profession of all. As a voluntary organization the congregation has the power to veto or undermine the best efforts of its pastor. Imagine what would happen to the effectiveness, say, of lawyers and physicians if they first had to win the votes of the vast majority of their clients or patients before they could proceed to represent or heal them. And further, suppose each week they had to perform before a public assembly of those clients and patients for their critical appraisal in order to win enough political support from that diverse population to continue to practice. God knows that people choose to work under these conditions only because divine persuasion prevails over common sense. But being bound to a voluntary organization is not the *most* difficult aspect of the profession.

Suppose the lawyer and the physician accepted the ordeal of weekly demonstrations of their crafts; at least they would know what to exhibit. The physician might display a recovered patient and the lawyer a client acquitted of the charges. The bedeviling thing about the ordained ministry is that the service it offers is so intangible. What is the effect for which ministry strives? Expanded church rolls and budget are of course the most common indices of the effectiveness of ministry. Clergy careers unfold on the basis of this institutional measure. But, clearly, this confuses means with ends. The institution is intended to be a means of ministry rather than its end, so how shall we measure what it is that the institution is supposed to effect in its ministry? The end of ministry is spiritual change in persons. Now we see why ministry is the most difficult profession. How are we to detect spiritual change in parishioners, let alone assess it? What specific change is it that ministry ought to effect?

It is just here that I hope this book will be of help to clergy. I can offer little help in the acquiring of skills to manage the church as a voluntary organization. But I maintain that the ordained ministry misfires most, not because we clergy lack managerial skills, but because we are vague about the ends for which we are managing. If we were clearer about the effects we seek in our ministries, we could capitalize on the considerable managerial skills most parish clergy already possess. It is this vagueness about the ends of ministry which is killing us—that and the absence of a strategy for ministry which greater clarity could bring.

I shall argue here that the fundamental aim of the ordained ministry is *to guide parishioners toward maturing in the Christian life*. This is a terribly intangible goal, to be sure, but we must not shrink from the task of describing it on that account. After all, that is what theologians are for —to deal with such intangibles. "No one has ever seen God," says John. Still, theologians seek to describe the Godhead. Maturing in the Christian life is at root maturing in relationship to this unseen God. That process of maturing is so difficult to describe because of this unseen and unseeable divine partner in the relationship. It would be understandable if to make the task easier we simply overlooked this unseen partner and described only the person we could see. That is a tempting out for a multitude of reasons, but it would be to default on the fundamental task before us. In terms of intellectual disciplines it would be to confuse psychology with theology.

It is just that confusion I wish to avoid by offering this biblical-theological version of faith development as an alternative to the psychological version offered by James W. Fowler in *Stages of Faith.* [1] When Fowler defines his subject matter as self, other, and shared centers of value and power, he overlooks the divine partner who makes the Christian life what it is. Only when the Godhead of Christian faith is taken fully into account do we have an adequate description of maturing in the Christian life and by the same token an adequate ground for a theology of the church's ministry.

Fowler is not to blame for avoiding the specifically theological task. He never intended to pursue it. The subtitle of his work offers fair warning of its limitations: *The Psychology of Human Development and the Quest for Meaning.* The confusion arises when clergy attempt to use this psychological perspective on human development as a substitute for a theological perspective on maturing in the Christian life. Fowler's work has no more applicability to Christian faith than it has to any other religious quest for meaning. Its proper application would be perhaps in a public education setting where separation of church and state prohibits endorsement of any particular faith commitment, or in an interfaith dialogue which seeks common denominators among different religions.

I do not mean to imply that a biblical-theological version of maturing in the Christian life is unrelated to psychologies of faith development. They share certain assumptions about the character of growth in persons of faith. But taking account of the particularities of Christ and the Holy Spirit produces very different estimates of what constitutes maturity. Faith in Christ does indeed embody itself in the psychosocial structures that psychologies of faith attempt to identify and describe. But faith in Christ reshapes the structures it inhabits, so that a psychology of religion in general is not likely to be adequate to the psychology of faith in Christ.

For example, the particularities of faith in Christ and the experience of the Holy Spirit produce very different estimates of what characterizes maturing. Fowler's scheme concentrates on the self's perceptions and values, while the New Testament account of faith soon requires a radical displacement of the self with the figure of Christ. In the most advanced stage of Fowler's scheme a certain leveling of faith objects occurs among different religions. Particular faith objects come to share in some common denominator. In the New Testament it is just the opposite. It is a mark of the crowd's very elemental and immature faith that they rank Jesus with a host of other religious figures such as John the Baptist, Elijah, or one of the prophets (Mark 8:28). In the most advanced phases of New Testament faith Jesus reigns as head of the universe in which there can be no comparable being (Col. 1:15ff.). Maturing in the Christian life involves a growing awareness of the exclusive and incomparable claim of Christ's Lordship over against the claims of all other possible objects of faith. It is beyond the scope of this book to undertake any careful comparison of maturing as the New Testament portrays it with the portrait of faith in Fowler's scheme. Let us all hope that an unfolding dialogue over faith development will sooner or later get to that task.

In any case, if you agree that the ordained ministry is responsible for fostering the whole ministry of a congregation, but is hamstrung by a voluntary organization and too vague an assignment, you might conclude that the only thing sure about the ministry is eventual burnout preceded by bouts of depression and demoralizing uncertainty. I do not so view it. Multitudes of clergy lead lives of quiet joyfulness and unheralded effectiveness. I do believe, however, that without a clearer picture of the maturing Christian they hope to nurture and a strategy to accompany that clearer picture, ministers are unfairly burdened in their work. It is the job of theologians to provide this clearer picture and to suggest a strategy in keeping with it. My prayer is that this book may offer some help in these regards to the end that the yoke of ministry may be eased and its burden lightened.

CHAPTER 1
AN INTEGRATING CENTER
FOR THE MINISTER'S WORK

Crisis at Mid-Career

Throughout their careers clergy experience the need for some perspective on their work that will help them to order the mind-boggling variety of demands their parishioners lay upon them. Without such ordering of priorities, the minister feels overloaded with details and unsure if the sixty-hour-plus workweek is yielding results to match the time and effort invested. Even more important to continuing morale is the need for some integrating center from which the minister can preserve a satisfying balance between what the church requires to satisfy the conditions of employment and what the minister requires to satisfy his or her sense of calling.

This need for an ordering and integrating center peaks periodically in typical clerical careers. The most frequently discussed time for clergy, as for many other professional groups, is mid-career. One Saturday morning amid the breakfast dishes and the litter of a week of parallel careers, I chanced upon a minister and his spouse. Their guards were down. He had been reading a book on mid-life crisis, geared especially to clergy. In it he found an excruciatingly accurate metaphor for the way he felt his life was going. It was in a section entitled "Just a Machine." The author is sharing his agony with his wife: "I said to Sally at one point, 'I feel like a vending machine, dispensing products. Someone pushes a button, and out comes a sermon. Someone pushes another button for a solution to a personal or administrative problem. The family pushes buttons, and out come dollars or time involvement. The community pushes other buttons, and I show up at meetings, sign petitions, and take stands.' "[2] My friend's lament was that he never got to push any buttons of his own choosing. His life seemed forever at the mercy of the bidding of others. My Saturday morning companion had grown bone weary satisfying the requirements of others, with no compensating chance to meet his own. He was like the member of a first-aid squad, forever at the mercy of those at-home radios, liable to squeal an emergency call at any minute. It was time to put in an emergency call of his own, but a one-way system set up for only incoming calls offered no way to call out.

The soft undertone of most such conversations includes the wish to change location, but at mid-career it is difficult to arrange for a next parish of comparable size and salary. Even then there is no guarantee that the same frustration will not unfold in the next place. My minister friend was highly successful in meeting all the requirements the congregation judges belong to his vocation, but he had no equivalent success in meeting the requirements for his own vocational satisfaction. If he was to maintain energy and élan for the second half of his career, he needed a more effective way to sort out and reconcile these two competing sets of requirements.

Crisis in the Beginning Years

This same minister had probably experienced a similar crisis early in his career, but it came at a time of life that receives much less public attention. Besides, he was much more resilient then. There is this other time in the ministry, however, when there is an acute need for a way to bring order and greater satisfaction to one's calling. It may be buried in memory, not by intervening successes, but by experiences too painful to permit recall. At least that is what mature clergy often report to me at conferences where we try to review some of the best and worst times of the first five years after graduation from seminary. In a study on stress in ministry, ministers reported that 42 percent of the periods of stress they recalled took place during the first five years, and more than 25 percent in the first two years.[3]

Donald Smith found that the major source of stress in the first years is the conflict between the image of the profession that the minister carries into it and the way the profession actually unfolds. Typically the new minister wishes to be a prophet-pastor, while the congregation looks for an administrator-pastor. Small first congregations want to flourish as institutions. New clergy want to bring the kingdom of God to persons and to society. I suspect that one of the reasons the stress peaks at two years is that by then the realization has dawned on the aspiring prophet that the congregation has more power to get what it wants from the new minister than the new minister has to get what he or she wants from the first congregation. As the novice clergyperson struggles for a more realistic appreciation of the demands of the profession, there is every chance that the institution will also force its agenda on him or her without due regard for the original urge to be a prophet-pastor. In the measure this happens, the unfortunate compromise struck in the early years will haunt the whole career until the frustration of that Saturday-morning conversation breaks out in later years. New clergy are usually strikingly successful at meeting the realities of the profession but disappointingly unsuccessful at meeting the realities of their own calling.

In denominations with an appointive system, the weight of this early period tilts too easily in favor of institutional needs and away from calling needs. Methodist clergy agreed that in those first years they felt like Sisyphus condemned perpetually to roll a huge stone up a high hill only to have the stone roll back down again.[4] In both the call system and the appointment system, beginning clergy tend to land in congregations that are so troubled or so marginal they cannot attract more skilled and experienced clergy.

Under an appointive system a minister's first congregation has probably been the victim of a rapid succession of inexperienced clergy who never stayed long enough to share the benefits of the experience won at the congregation's expense. No wonder the congregation has little enthusiasm for the next clerical leader's idea of ministry. Sooner or later the novice appointee awakens to the truth that few in the congregation or in the supervising hierarchy expect much accomplishment in terms of ministry. The real assignment is to learn to get along in the institution by going along with its needs as an institution. What the denominational supervisor wants to see is how cheerfully new clergy accept an assignment where the stone regularly rolls back down and over the struggling prophet-pastor. If during the testing period the new minister bounces up again smiling and cheerful after each traverse of the rock, he or she shows promise of deserving a next post where some accomplishment is possible. During the same period the new clergyperson may observe that the larger organization has few means to monitor prophetic-pastoral ministry, but many indices of how well things are going for the institution. This whole set of initial circumstances tends to present the profession as one that requires an adjustment that is both unfair and unsatisfying to the neophyte's sense of calling.

Sometimes institutional needs upstage the calling even

in the process of recognizing that call. I know a young woman seminarian whose approval for ordination was postponed for a year with the explanation by the examining committee that they knew she could stand the postponement better than other, less mature candidates.

If theological education does its job well, new clergy come from seminary fired with the mission to be agents of change. No wonder they suffer trauma when they discover *they* are the chief targets of change. The tragedy is not that new clergy need to change their perception of the ministry, but that currently neither the seminaries nor the churches offer a metaphor for ministry that stands up under the first excruciating tension between the needs of one's calling and the needs of the church as institution.

One of the chief aims of this book is to provide such a metaphor. In my judgment the trauma of the early years arises not from having to come to terms with the realities of the profession but from the sense of having to surrender one's dream of ministry in the process. As the institution presents its claims on the profession, too little allowance is made for the element of prophet-pastor. If it were just that this dream were being given better orientation to reality, that would not be so bad. What feels bad is that the prophet-pastor seems eclipsed. The seeds for mid-career despair are sown when, looking back, we see that so much of the calling seems to have been neglected.

Crisis in the Final Years

The bearable thing about the crises of integrity that often occur in early and mid career is that there is still time to compensate for what seems to be going or has gone amiss in the working out of the minister's calling. But what is to be done when retirement draws near and there is no time to correct for lost dreams? More than one mature clergyperson has said to me, "If I had only known all this forty years sooner!"

If my metaphor for ministry is apt, it should not only inform the life of the minister in full swing, but it should encompass the whole span of ministry. It is one of the virtues of a metaphor for ministry tied to organic development that it can provide for every time, no matter how we may sigh to ourselves or the world declare that the chances of renewed meaning lie behind us. The metaphor for ministry we seek should stand up at every time of career, clarifying and encouraging the ministry at hand.

Outworn Metaphors for Ministry

H. Richard Niebuhr's famous metaphor for the minister as "pastoral director,"[5] and more recent variations of it,[6] continue to be useful in taking account of the two elements that distinguish the ministry from other professions, namely, the sense of a personal calling to be a prophetic resource to persons and to structures in society plus accountability to an organization that the minister both leads and serves. But this metaphor merely juxtaposes the two elements. What is missing in "pastoral director" is just the integrative element we are seeking. We require some perspective that can order the various role demands the institution places on the minister as well as balance personal calling and institutional accountability.

Samuel Blizzard described exactly the thing we are seeking. It is what Donald Smith and he call a minister's "integrative role." Speaking from a time when clergy were expected to be male, the integrative role is the minister's "goal orientation, or frame of reference to his work. . . . It is the end toward which he is working in his professional relationship with parishioners, church associations, community groups, and the general public. It is what he is trying to accomplish with people in the professional practice of religion."[7]

The closest Niebuhr came to offering such a goal orientation was to suggest that the work of the pastoral-director is "the increase among men of the love of God and Neighbor." The value of this formulation is that it makes room for the two major foci for ministry within Protestantism: evangelism and social action or to use the language of the recent report of the Association of Theological Schools, "spiritual emphasis" and "social action emphasis."[8]

The churches have just completed two decades devoted to each of these emphases in turn, the 1960s for social action and the 1970s for evangelism. A historical and theological analysis of one or the other of these emphases shows each to be wanting as an adequate expression of the ministry.[9] In the measure to which these are used to focus ministry in turn or together, the result has proved to be unresolvable conflict within a congregation or a denomination.[10] In the pluralistic churches of today, both emphases are always present to some extent, so that the ideal ministry attempts some balance between the two.

This balance as the goal for ministry has produced the latest attempts to epitomize the work of the minister in terms of the master roles[11] of "facilitator," "enabler," and "conflict manager." In a pluralistic church the first two lead inevitably to the last. If the minister undertakes to encourage and implement the crazy-quilt variety of ideas in the average congregation of what the church should be doing with its members and resources, he or she soon finds that these ideas are competitive rather than complementary. At that point the presiding pastor must become a "conflict manager" or the whole operation dissolves into political chaos.

An apt metaphor for this very popular form of integrative role for ministry today would be the forest ranger on watch high up in a fire tower. The task of the minister is

constantly to survey the horizon of the parish and be alert
for any sign of impending conflict. Under this metaphor,
the good minister is the one who keeps reducing the
elapsed time from the detection of the first wisp of the
smoke of conflict, through the scramble down the long
ladder and the rush out to the trouble spot, to the stamp-
ing out of the smoldering source of smoke before it bursts
into the flame of serious congregational conflict. As a master role this is, to say the least, wearing. Worst of all, it is
hopeless as a means of satisfying calling, since it puts us
back into that vending machine experience, completely at
the disposal of the initiative and expectation of others,
with no space left to satisfy one's own sense of calling.

The effect of facilitator, enabler, and conflict manager as
master roles tends to be a bland and temporary peace at
the expense of any unifying and energizing vision. The
roles of enabler and conflict manager discourage any prophetic input from the minister. An enabler serves others'
vision; a conflict manager does not complicate the scene
with one more contending point of view. Actually these
master roles are more appropriate to the therapeutic community from which they came. They serve to provide a
kind of peace and unity in the church but not the purity
that distinguishes the church from other groups in society.

There is some theological sense in the notion that the
church models reconciliation in a pluralistic society by
helping all kinds of people to get along together in church
who would not associate, let alone work together in the
world outside the church. This is the argument that is
offered as a theological justification for the minister in the
dominant roles of enabler and conflict manager. But reconciliation in the New Testament means primarily reconciliation to God and transformation of persons who then
work for transformation in the world—not carte blanche
provision for whatever views and life-styles members
bring to congregational life.

Thus, reconciliation among Christians means living, working, and worshiping together on a basis that transcends the common denominator that conflict management finds. Unless this transforming and transcending reconciliation sets the tone, life in the church merely mirrors the tensions of pluralistic society. Reconciliation as transformation calls for ministerial leadership with a vision that transcends the conflict between evangelicals and social activists. The function of providing a transforming vision that transcends conflicting parties is not adequately included under "enabler" or "conflict manager." That is why we are searching beyond them for a metaphor for ministry with such a vision. We need a way of doing ministry that catches up what is most valuable in each of the two dominant parties of American Christianity and reconciles their adherents at a new level beyond the present competition between them. The metaphor for minister as such a visionary will include the functions of enabler and conflict manager, since those skills will always be appropriate to leaders of voluntary organizations. But when reconciliation is defined in terms of transformation, the result we hope for within the churches is more than an uneasy truce in the ongoing cold war between baptized Democrats and Republicans.

As we have reviewed the major integrating perspectives upon ministry of the past few decades, it has become increasingly clear what we seek. We need a metaphor to meet the crises of ministerial identity that occur typically in the early years, at mid-career, and in the years before retirement. This implies that the metaphor will need to have developmental relevance to the whole life span. We need a metaphor that also features a master or integrative role that lets the clergyperson know with greater specificity what he or she is trying to accomplish through the usual professional roles of preacher, liturgist, pastor, educator, evangelist, advocate of justice, and administrator.

The generalized aim to spread the love of God and neighbor is too vague.[12] The metaphor should also provide a reference by which the minister can strike a satisfying balance between what the congregation wants of the minister and what the minister needs in order to satisfy a sense of calling. It must also provide a vision of the mission of the church and its ministry that transcends the polarity and party spirit of evangelical-conservative versus social activist-liberal, private party versus public party. It will be the thesis of this book that *prophetic guide to maturing in the Christian life* is a metaphor for the professional ministry that fulfills all these specifications.

Prophetic Guide

When we first hear this metaphor it may seem to be suggesting a retreat into sectarian piety divorced from concern for social justice. The prophetic note in the metaphor should allay that anxiety, for it points to the vision of social justice that maturing in the Christian life entails. In fact the metaphor of prophetic guide draws its substance from the content of the Christian life to which it points. The Christian life I find described in the New Testament culminates in a willingness to engage in mission that includes witness, acts of charity, and acts of justice—all at risk of losing worldly reward. The note of risk is essential, for it reflects the biblical dimension of self-denial and tragedy symbolized in the cross. This distinguishes Christian maturing from the upward mobility so often associated with evangelism, and from the triumphalism so often associated with social action. While confirming social concern, this metaphor at the same time confirms the concern for true piety so dear to the hearts of evangelicals.

It even makes room for a third concern within Christendom, namely, the emphasis on Spirit in the charismatic movement. A New Testament doctrine of the Christian life provides for the element of spiritual giftedness so necessary to the exercise of mission in a graceful way. At the same time, it provides grounds for a sympathetic critique of the charismatic movement's foibles, as well as of the foibles of evangelicals and social activists. In short, I intend to give to this metaphor for the ministry content out of a doctrine of the Christian life that includes the best of each major contemporary version of the Christian in mission. In no way does prophetic guide simply confirm the status quo in the world or in the church.

The master role to which this metaphor points declares that the main business of clergy is to provide or arrange for the resources necessary for Christians to mature. I will illustrate in a final chapter how this master role as a metaphor for integration can direct the energy of the pastoral leader in each of the professional roles. But at the outset it is important to see the metaphor of prophetic guide as the source of professional identity. The minister is unique compared with all the other helping professionals by virtue of the unique outcomes of his or her labor. The end result of the work of the clergy is maturing Christians. Over time in any place the effectiveness of ministry may be judged by the signs of maturing among parishioners.

This particular function of the pastoral leader is what gives the ministry its special identity. It may share a spectrum of functions with other helping professions engaged in social work, medicine, or psychological counseling, but no other profession is equipped to see to maturing in the Christian life. Once the ministry comes to realize its unique contribution to human life, it can reclaim its place at the head of the professions—not because other professions grant this, but because ministers know that their work is the most crucial service one human being can offer another. The ministry points the way to the pearl of great price.

This is not to say that the prophetic guide deals only

with individuals. Christians mature in company with each other, so that the guide always conducts a group tour. What is more, the church in mission focuses on social systems as well as on individuals. The doctrine of the Christian life that underlies the metaphor of prophetic guide will suggest that effectiveness in ministry may be measured not only by the quality of life of individuals but also by the kinds of groups the minister's efforts generate and by the effect they have on the surrounding community in the world.

This metaphor for ministry applies as much to the life of the minister as to the life of the parishioner. In particular, our doctrine of the Christian life provides guidance at every stage of the minister's career and sets the context for a ministry to ministers in the common crises of early, mid, and late career. We shall see that clerical careers tend to unfold in predictable stages just as research suggests is characteristic of all adult life. This raises the question of the relevance of developmental models to a doctrine of the Christian life. Do developmental models for adult life suggest that a doctrine of the Christian life should follow a similar scheme?

An Alternative to a Developmental Approach to the Christian Life

The most popular theory of faith development is the one being offered by James W. Fowler in *Stages of Faith*.[13] My approach differs significantly from his. Fowler's method is to interview many subjects for their story of faith. My method will be to look for the stories of faith portrayed in the New Testament. Fowler fashions his categories for analyzing and classifying stories of faith from Piaget's theory of cognitive development, Kohlberg's theory of moral development, and Erikson's psychosocial development. These theories reflect evolutionary assumptions about organic life which determine the picture of the life of faith. The result of these assumptions is that faith unfolds as a one-way journey. It proceeds through six successive stages on a gradient from lower to higher forms until the most mature self arrives at a universalizing stage completing the development. In this final state a radical commitment to pluralism relativizes all particular faith stances so that none are excluded.

The ruling assumption seems to be that the human self is programmed in some paragenetic way to seek meaning by ever more appropriate adaptation to an ever-enlarging environment. This evolutionary adaptation comes to a climax when it is universal in its sympathies and tolerant of every particular religious tradition by virtue of the "Unconditioned" that comes to expression in all religions. Although the path of development is predetermined, any particular self may cease developing and stick at conventional levels. The track is predetermined, but the degree of progression on it is not.

My way of giving structure to the Christian life shares with faith development the ideas of stages or eras and a particular sequence to them, but that is all. As I read the New Testament, the life of faith is drawn ahead by the Spirit rather than driven from behind by the self. Indeed, so long and insofar as the journey is driven by the self, faith is inauthentic. The self's idea of faith is so laced with illusion that its quest must be displaced by the Spirit's drawings in order for authentic faith to emerge and mature. In the Christian life there is no completion of the journey in this life under the conditions of this world. Maturity comes finally in a new body in the setting of a new heaven and a new earth. In this life we are ever in the process of maturing; we never arrive.

While the sequence of eras or stages is given by the promise of the creature in a new creation and by the Spirit's drawings toward fulfillment of that promise, they are not experienced as separate stages. Instead they are phases or dimensions of a wholistic experience that moves back and forth along a spectrum, appropriating and emphasizing now this phase, now that. I prefer the word "phase" to "stage" or "era" because of this more fluid interrelationship among phases. From a sequential point of view no phase is ever left behind but is caught up in the next as its necessary ground. The metaphor of a temple that grows as if it were a body is apt (Eph. 2:20–21). The advantages of this metaphor are the combining of elements of structure (apostles and prophets as the foundation, Christ Jesus as the cornerstone), sequence (from foundation to complete temple), and organic growth (the whole structure is joined together and grows).

But given the importance of sequence, the movement within is neither necessary nor one way. A person may decide not to have faith or, having had faith, to recant (Heb. 6:1–8), or, having had faith and matured some in it, to regress (Gal. 3:3). These options for the Christian life seem to fall outside development in an evolutionary sense.

Fowler calls his frame of understanding for faith "structural-developmental." I would call mine "phased-eschatological," with the phases experienced both as in sequence and simultaneous. Such descriptions are only suggestive and a little pretentious. We shall see what they mean when we come to the matter itself. I only wish at this point to serve notice that faith development theory as developed by Fowler does not describe what I find in the New Testament. In theological terms I see Fowler's system or design as a variation of redemptive history with its chronological sequence of dispensations. It has an existentialist twist as well in its tendency to reduce particular religious traditions to subjectivity. Piaget and Kohlberg give Fowler structure for this subjectivity, just as Heidegger gave Bultmann structure for his reduction of Christian tradition.

In short, faith development strikes me as an existentialist version of redemptive history in which history is reduced to personal response while holding fast to a chronological framework. The final picture is of a religious self telling its beads of meaning on a rosary of time. This psychology of the pious self completely obscures the majesty of God. The New Testament keeps an eye on the religious self, to be sure, but overshadows it with the majesty of God. I seek to follow that distribution of emphasis in my portrayal of the Christian life. The final picture that the New Testament offers loses the religious self in "a great multitude which no one can number, . . . standing before the throne and before the Lamb, . . . crying out with a loud voice, 'Salvation belongs to our God who sits upon the throne, and to the Lamb!' While a surrounding choir of angels responds 'Amen! Blessing and glory and wisdom and thanksgiving and honor and power and might be to our God for ever and ever! Amen' " (Rev. 7:9–10). That is somewhat different from faith development's culminating reverence for the religious self at stage six!

The Christian Life, the Adult Life Cycle, and the Church Year

For me there is pressing need for conversation that distinguishes the Christian life from other faith options and especially from the patterns being offered by contemporary culture. We are just now discovering what this patterning is like. Gail Sheehy gives a journalist's report of this research in her best seller, *Passages.*[14] Daniel Levinson gives his report of fundamental research on men through mid-life in *The Seasons of a Man's Life* (a similar report on women is to follow).[15] What these and comparable investigations show is that there are predictable stages and transitions in adult life just as we know there are for children. Many parents are able to survive parenting only because of the assurance that the outrageous behavior of their child is merely a stage in its development and that with patience, firmness, and understanding, the child will return to the world of civilized behavior. The same perilous odyssey continues into adulthood.

For adults, these unfolding stages and transitions are as heavily programmed by cultural expectations as by the biological and psychological factors that determine childhood. There is research to show that the rhythm of the lives of adult men and women in our society is determined largely by career patterns at work and expectations of self-fulfillment, especially sexual fulfillment, in their personal lives. Compared with these, any specifically religious value orientation seems to count for little. Unless these clearly powerful and increasingly well defined influences on the lives of church members are met by equally powerful and well-defined influences of grace for living the Christian life, the role of clergy is in danger of being reduced to the role of chaplains, summoned for brief, emergency ministrations to a life cycle unfolding in complete isolation from the life of faith.

It is time for the church to reassert its guidance in the lives of its adult members, for they are as much at the mercy of a captivating culture as were the members of the early church before the invention of the church year. In ancient culture the peak times of the agricultural and solar years, such as spring planting, fall harvest, winter solstice, and spring equinox, threatened to seduce the people of God to the worship of fertility and sun gods and goddesses connected with these peak times. Israel pioneered churchly guidance and protection of its people by displacing the festivals of Canaanite culture with festivals marking the history of Israel's redemption as a people. The church followed suit (for different reasons) by displacing the Jewish festivals with Good Friday, Easter, and Pentecost, and the pagan winter festival of the sun-god with

Advent. Until the church of our time finds alternate, graceful ways to mark the Christian life of adults, the sad secular holidays of mid-life crisis—retirement, aging, and finally death and dying—will cast a spell over the lives of Christians. Just as the invention of the church year broke the spell of the gods of sun, moon, and stars, so now the recovery of a clear-cut doctrine of the Christian life must break the spell of the all too predictable pattern of adult life.

The Rise of the Charismatic Movement

Recent theological reflection has not served the churches well in furnishing a theory of the life of a Christian to place over against the culture's cycle of adult life. One might have expected that the redemptive history school of biblical theology would have gone on to apply its linear, periodizing scheme to Christian experience. It did not, because, like neo-orthodoxy to which it was related, it was shy of experience and hostile to the Bultmannian call to construct a hermeneutical bridge from the Bible to the novel situation of our time. Especially in its Barthian form, neo-orthodoxy was wary of "mysticism," pietism, and experience-centered theologies of the nineteenth century. It was so bound not to separate sanctification from justification or to erect an "order of salvation" that no comprehensive frame of understanding was given to sanctification.

Dietrich Bonhoeffer's classic was as close as neo-orthodoxy ever got to a doctrine of the Christian life, but *The Cost of Discipleship (Nachfolge)* was mainly an exposition of the Sermon on the Mount and of Matthew 10. It ignored the description of the Christian life in the balance of the New Testament. And so it was that academic theology's most recent reflection on the Christian life has been so shy of offering guides for experience that it has left the field wide open to the pietism it intended to combat. The chief legacy of Bonhoeffer is the term "discipleship," which has become the designation in mainline Protestant denominations for the whole Christian life.

Neo-orthodoxy practically fostered neo-Pentecostalism by its neglect of Christian experience. Theology, like nature, abhors a vacuum. The piety that has filled the vacuum since the early 1960s came to be called the charismatic movement. Its origins lie in the evangelical revival in England and especially in Wesley's doctrine of perfection. In the famous Aldersgate experience, Wesley found the sudden assurance of salvation that the Moravians promised. But it was the next experience, also sudden, for which his movement became famous, what Albert Outler calls the "fullness of faith" and what Wesley called "perfection."[16]

Outler is correct in praising Wesley for his concern that the revivalist's work was not done when he had mediated conversion. In what is perhaps the last classic Protestant treatment of sanctification, Bunyan's *The Pilgrim's Progress,* Christian is converted one sixth of the way through the book and the balance is devoted to his pilgrimage. In the tradition of revivalism and mass evangelism in America, however, so much attention was given to conversion that the other five sixths of the convert's life were simply neglected, with the result that most converts aborted their pilgrimage near its beginning. Although we must congratulate Wesley and his descendants on their concern for sanctification, they tended to focus it, like conversion, on a single experience at a point in time. Perfection soon became the next experience to be pursued beyond conversion.

In the late nineteenth century, the pursuit of perfection amounted to an obsession in American churches. But as mainline denominations moved away from dependence on revivals and mass evangelism, they came to apply the

optimism of perfection more to the arena of social transformation than to the sphere of personal sanctification.[17]
The result was that Methodist devotion to entire sanctification had to find expression outside the denomination in
so-called Holiness groups. These eventually spawned Pentecostalism.[18]

The Pentecostal idea of a "second blessing," marked by
speaking in tongues, has now returned to influence American churches of every stripe in the form of the charismatic
movement.[19] The idea of speaking in tongues is highly
disturbing to the vast majority of pastoral leaders because
it puts them in an impossible bind. The practice claims
support from Paul, who explicitly bans its prohibition (I
Cor. 14:39), and from Acts, but its advocates offer no doctrine of the Christian life by which this experience can be
integrated into so-called normal parish life. The result is
that the average pastoral leader feels bound to grant the
biblical precedent but compelled to resist its practice.
Without a doctrine of the Christian life to make sense of
speaking in tongues, there is no way to integrate it into the
normal life of a noncharismatic congregation.

The charismatic movement is but the latest instance of
a syndrome that repeats itself in the life of the church.
When the pastoral leader has no clearly defined understanding of the Christian life as an ongoing experience,
someone else will fill that vacuum with exotic substitutes
profoundly disturbing to pastor and people alike. Clerical
fishers of men and women need some standard to determine which fish to keep and which to return to the stream.

Biblical Grounds for the Metaphor
of Prophetic Guide

The New Testament does not display an office of minister comparable to the pastoral leader of our institutional-
ized church.[20] It does offer a variety of figures whose pro-

phetic function provides a model for the office of ministry
today. Prophecy, in the sense of declaration of the mighty
act of God in Christ for salvation, anchored the life of the
people of God then as it does now. This fact is symbolized
by the career of John the Baptist, the prophetic forerun-
ner of Jesus' ministry. Jesus himself appeared to be a
prophet before messianic appreciation of him took over
(Mark 8:28; Luke 24:19). Paul reflected the primacy of
prophecy by rating it above all the other gifts of the Spirit
which provide for ministry in his congregations (I Cor.
14:1, 5, 24, 31, 39). This prominence of prophecy continued in the Pauline school in the ranking of prophecy
second among the gifts after apostleship (Eph. 4:11). It is
assumed that prophets guide the life of the church in Acts,
although they are thrown in the background by the
Twelve (Acts 11:27ff; 15:32; 21:10). For Luke, Paul was not
an apostle in the sense of the Twelve, but was numbered
among others as a prophet and teacher (Acts 13:1).

Our interest in prophecy is to discover the master role
or major effect intended. It is striking that in Zechariah's
meditation upon his newborn son's role as prophet, the
culminating function was "to guide our feet into the way
of peace" (Luke 1:79), making John the original prophetic
guide. Luke wrote late enough that the immediate expectation of the end had been displaced by reckoning with
the long haul of history and, most significantly for our
purposes, with the long haul of the Christian life. Zechariah's "way of peace" introduced Luke's conception of
Christianity as "the Way" (Acts 9:2; 19:9; 24:22). Luke's
special interest in journeys invites us to see his description
of the Christian life as a metaphor for a phased journey
which it is the ministry of the prophets to "strengthen"
(Acts 15:32).

Paul also modeled this guiding function of prophecy.
As an apostle he distinguished his ministry from that of
others by virtue of having been the originating parent of

faith for congregations (I Cor. 3:10–17; Rom. 15:20) and individuals (I Cor. 4:15). This means that he was not content merely to initiate faith and then leave its nurture to others. When he wrote to the Corinthians claiming to be their father in the faith in contrast to "countless guides in Christ," he was functioning through the letters precisely as a guide to improve on the work of other guides. Indeed he saw himself as a parent whose ultimate function was to bring his charges to maturity by building up (I Thess. 5:11; I Cor. 10:23; 14:12; II Cor. 10:8; 13:10), edifying (I Cor. 14:4, 26; Rom. 15:2), and upbuilding (Rom. 14:19; I Cor. 14:3; II Cor. 12:19), all words with the same Greek root.[21]

The Pauline school caught the same master role for ministry and continued it in terms of parenting (Eph. 4:14), growth (Eph. 4:15), building up (Eph. 4:12, 16; Col. 2:6–7), edification (Eph. 4:29), and maturing (Eph. 4:13; Col. 1: 28–29; 4:12). Churches and individuals are temples of the Holy Spirit in process of construction (Eph. 2:20–22). The main task of apostolic and prophetic ministry is to serve that process of construction. The climactic expression of maturing in the Christian life as the ultimate aim of all ministry in the church comes in Ephesians:

> And his gifts were that some should be apostles, some prophets, some evangelists, some pastors and teachers, to equip the saints for the work of ministry, for building up the body of Christ, until we all attain to the unity of the faith and of the knowledge of the Son of God, to mature manhood, to the measure of the stature of the fulness of Christ. . . . We are to grow up in every way into him who is the head, into Christ, from whom the whole body, joined and knit together by every joint with which it is supplied, when each part is working properly, makes bodily

growth and upbuilds itself in love. (Eph. 4:11–
16)

This is a prose ode to the master role of ministry as prophetic guide to maturing in the Christian life. Other New
Testament authors reinforce this perspective on ministry.

The author of the Fourth Gospel featured this same
function under the metaphor of shepherd. Jesus modeled
that metaphor in John 10 and then passed it on to Peter
as his dominant role after resurrection (John 21:15–17).
The shepherd is responsible for protecting the sheep
against error, but the ultimate function is to nourish their
growth. The shepherd metaphor also occurs: in Matthew,
for Jesus' ministry (Matt. 9:36; 15:24) and for that of the
Twelve (10:6); in I Peter for the ministry of the elders and
of Christ (I Peter 5:2ff.); and in Acts (20:28–29). Our word
"pastor" is the English form of shepherd. I Peter 2:25 and
Acts 20:28 connect bishop with the functioning of a shepherd to emphasize protection against error.

Finally, the church chose Paul as a model for institutional ministry. The Pastorals present the mature Paul
parenting his charges and fellow workers Timothy (I Tim.
1:1–2; II Tim. 1:1–2) and Titus (1:1, 4). Titus epitomized
the apostolic function in nurturing and developmental
terms that confirm the central role of prophetic guide to
maturing in the Christian life: "Paul, a servant of God and
an apostle of Jesus Christ, to further the faith of God's elect
and their knowledge of the truth which accords with god-
liness" (1:1).

Summary

The New Testament justifies our metaphor for ministry
insofar as may be reasonably expected. Given the near
expectation of the end and the temporary character of life
in the early church, it is surprising how much account is

taken of the necessity to nurture the church and its members to maturity in a process that takes time. With this much encouragement, we move to the embryo doctrine of the Christian life that emerges in the New Testament. Even in embryo form it gives enough content to "prophetic guide" to confirm the value of the metaphor. When we see how maturing in the Christian life works out in contemporary institutional terms, we shall see the prophetic note come to full clarity. At this point it is enough to be encouraged that the metaphor has a New Testament basis, speaks to the predictable crises of clergy careers, and brings integrity to the impossibly broad spectrum of role expectation laid on the profession by congregation and ministry alike. Finally, the doctrine of the Christian life contained in the metaphor will offer a gracious alternative to the fateful adult life cycle we see our culture fastening onto us all.

CHAPTER 2
THE DISCIPLESHIP PHASE
OF THE CHRISTIAN LIFE

Discipleship Redefined

In spite of current usage, I am making discipleship only a phase of the Christian life rather than a description of the whole. The root word for discipleship comes from the Greek verb *akoloutheō*, "to follow," as in the command of Jesus, "Follow me." The emphasis lies on the action of following Jesus and on the relationship of personal attachment to him that following entails. Our word "disciple" comes from a different word, *mathētēs*, whose meaning is "learner" or "pupil." Jesus did indeed act as a teacher to disciples as students, but the relationship between him and his followers was much more crucial than that of a student to a rabbi. In the relationship with a rabbi the emphasis was on the subject matter. In the relationship with Jesus the emphasis was on Jesus himself. The kingdom about which he taught drew near not because he taught about it but because he embodied it. Therefore I want the word "disciple" to connote primarily attachment to the person of Jesus as it does in the Gospels rather than attention to a body of learning on the part of a student. Professor Fitzmyer puts it precisely in connection with his discussion of Luke: "Christian discipleship is portrayed not only as acceptance of a master's teaching, but as identification of oneself with the master's way of life and destiny in an intimate, personal following of him."[22]

The figure to follow is Jesus of Nazareth. Consequently, when we look for models and descriptions of the life of faith under the rubric of discipleship, we are confined almost entirely to the four Gospels, where the disciples spend a maximum of three years of their journey of faith. Most of that amounts to only puzzled beginnings of a faith which uniformly collapses under the weight of the crucifixion. To be sure, the resurrection revives that faith, but, except for Luke, the chroniclers of these beginnings offer no subsequent record of the disciples as followers of Jesus.

The New Testament story of faith's continuation after its initial collapse has to be gleaned from other books of the New Testament. In these books, for the most part, the journey of faith is not portrayed as following. When scholars look for a comparable single term for the life of faith after Easter, they come up with "imitate" as the sequel to "follow."[23]

Luke continues to call the faithful "disciples" in his second volume, but that is merely a carryover from his first volume. After the ascension there is no figure to follow, since Jesus stands at God's right hand (Acts 7:56). If there is anyone to follow, according to Acts, it would be the Spirit whom Jesus has poured out to bless and guide the church (Acts 2:33).[24]

Aside from Luke, only John and Matthew offer any continuing version of discipleship, but in very restricted ways. John portrays a risen Christ twice instructing Peter to follow him (John 21:19–22), but no figure is offered within that metaphor for him to follow. In John we are caught between a later editor's desire to continue the metaphor of discipleship and the original author's intention to close it off. The burden of the original author's farewell discourse was that Jesus would be absent from the disciples after his ascension and that the coming of the Holy Spirit as paraclete would fill the void. In her function as para-clete, the Spirit was positioned differently than Jesus had been.[25] The departing Jesus says that during the disciple-ship stage the Spirit "dwells with you" but afterward "will be in you." So the original author did not conceive of the Spirit as going before the disciples in some fashion analo-gous to Jesus' leading the disciples in the days of his flesh. That leaves Matthew as the remaining source for con-tinuation of the metaphor of discipleship beyond resurrec-tion.

The Great Commission appears to express this intention with, "Make disciples of all nations" (Matt. 28:19). When we inquire about the content of this discipleship, the an-swer is, "Teaching them to observe all that I have com-manded you." Presumably Jesus continues with the disci-ples through his commandments—"and lo, I am with you always, to the close of the age" (v. 20). It is hinted obliquely in the threefold formula for baptism that the Holy Spirit provides an added dimension to this continuation of disci-pleship. Presumably this baptism fulfills the promise of John that Jesus would baptize with the Holy Spirit and with fire (Matt. 3:11).

Two very important factors complicate Matthew's con-tinuing form of discipleship. From resurrection on, Jesus is with them, whereas before, they had been with Jesus, i.e., he had led out ahead of them. Where is the dynamic leadership of the itinerating Jesus after Easter? How does the Holy Spirit supply this dynamic if that is one of her intended functions? *Matthew supplies no answer to these questions.* Without further answers to these questions the mandate to teach "them to observe all that I have com-manded you" overshadows trinitarian baptism and the promise of Jesus' continuing presence. The result is that following Jesus tends to degenerate into following his ver-sion of the law. Discipleship becomes scarcely distinguish-able from Judaism. Jesus as the new Moses interprets the

law without concession to human hardness of heart (Matt.
19:8) but with concessions to rabbinic argumentation (v.
9). Christianity becomes another school of legal interpretation alongside the schools of Hillel and Shammai. To be
sure, this mode of being Christian is authentic but it misses
too much of what came to distinguish Christianity from
Judaism. I maintain that the church assembled a canon to
include literature that would answer the questions Matthew left unanswered. Until the journeying Christian
learns how to apply these answers he or she is caught in
a relatively early phase of faith maturing.

I do not mean to leave out of account the redaction
critical insight that Matthew, Mark, and particularly John
intended the episodes of Jesus' ministry to apply to the
present. It is a well-acknowledged assumption of Gospel
research that the materials of Jesus' ministry were pre-
served and retold precisely because the church experienced in them the continuing presence of the risen
Christ in the guise of a past figure.[26] Experiencing Christ's
presence in these Gospels is a major part of what it means
for them to become the Word of God. Nevertheless Christians who live primarily out of the discipleship metaphor
tend to be limited in their maturing by the tendency to
view the Gospel materials as stories of a past and absent
Master.

To sum up: Matthew, Mark, Luke, and John all portray
Christian faith in terms of discipleship up until the resurrection. Matthew recommends that metaphor as valid to
the close of the age, but does not give content for Jesus'
continuing presence. How baptism in the name of Father,
Son, and Holy Spirit makes a difference is never spelled
out.

In spite of the fact that its post-Easter content is vague,
very many Christians continue to be drawn to discipleship
as a term for being Christian in preference to other options offered within the canon. Why do so many prefer this

metaphor in spite of its vagueness when other New Testament metaphors for the Christian life seem better designed to fill the space left by the risen Christ? I certainly do not understand all the reasons but I suspect that some of the following are part of the answer.

The Appeal of Discipleship

One of the things that characterizes modern consciousness is its confidence that the critical study of history is a way to test the truth of traditional wisdom. This consistently critical appraisal of traditional wisdom is relatively recent. It only came to bear fully on the study of Christianity in the last quarter of the last century. Applied to Christianity it meant sooner or later the testing of the figure of Jesus Christ. With historical fact as the touchstone, a distinction immediately arose between Jesus of Nazareth, a known figure of history, and the risen Christ of faith, a figure beyond history. The only sure historical component to the risen Christ was the historicity of those who believed in him. Believing in this Christ amounted to having faith in someone else's faith. To avoid being vulnerable to all sorts of historically questionable myths, it seemed wise to turn to the firmer ground of Jesus of Nazareth. Thus one of the first projects of Christian scholars under the spell of history as the final arbiter of reality was the quest for the historical Jesus. As Albert Schweitzer's chronicle makes clear, this quest was driven not simply by the search for the holy grail of reliable historical fact, but also by the desire to undo in the name of Jesus a great deal of seeming nonsense that had clothed itself in the mantle of Christian dogma.[27]

These twin drives, to ground faith in history and to free us from dogma, still have their appeal today. It certainly takes a greater leap of faith for a modern historian to relate to the risen Christ of Pauline mysticism or to the paraclete of John than to commit oneself to the straightforward teaching and example of the historical Jesus. It takes far less credulity to remember this Jesus respectfully than it does to pray to him as a living presence. This form of faith protects one from certain excesses of religion brought on by mystical attachment to a risen Christ. For example, it is comforting to know that Jesus never spoke in tongues or that Jesus seemed more at home in the world of women, weddings, and wine than Paul ever was.

The wing of American Christianity that is concerned with social justice and attuned to theology in a modern idiom finds confirmation in the figure of Jesus. His prophetic message with its central theme of the kingdom of God blends with this party's commitment to justice and its concern for the poor and oppressed. As prophet of the coming kingdom Jesus ranks alongside the classic Old Testament prophets who are the chief patrons of this party. The Christ mysticism of Paul seems much more difficult to translate into modern myth than does the ethical religion of Jesus.

I suspect also that discipleship has great appeal to healthy, confident moderns. Jesus seemed to foster self-reliance, initiative, and responsibility. When he taught and directed others, he assumed they had the power to carry out his commands without debilitating reservations arising from doctrines of original sin and moral depravity. When, for example, Jesus told the parable of the good Samaritan he concluded with, "Go and do likewise" (Luke 10:37). That is something a healthy person can grasp. The Sermon on the Mount may not be easy, but it is understandable and many people under the constant pressure of the marketplace find it a steadying guide in that jungle of ethical relativity. There is less dependency in discipleship focused as it is on a healthy ability to respond rather than on the spiritual mysteries of a Paul or a John who harp on the inabilities of the sickly soul.

Surely these are some of the appeals of discipleship. Pastors charged with leading people committed to this mode of being Christian may find these musings helpful in imagining what forms of communication and program will appeal to devotees of discipleship. If clergy ever feel inclined to lead some kind of modern-day, religious equivalent of a charge up San Juan Hill, discipleship Christians are likely to be the rough riders who will want to form behind them. Discipleship breeds heroes of faith like Dietrich Bonhoeffer and Martin Luther King, Jr. This heroic note suggests the first feature of this initial phase of the process of Christian maturing.

The Motto of Discipleship

When we look for the New Testament model for discipleship, we find its archetype in the Twelve whom Jesus selected to be his closest companions and pupils. We concentrate on Mark's portrayal because Mark was the original artist and also because Matthew and Luke soften and touch up Mark's stark sketch. It is important at the outset to grant that the portraits of the disciples are drawn more to describe a phase of faith than to show what the Twelve were really like. The quest of the historical disciples, like the quest of the historical Jesus, leads us as much to theologies of faith of the synoptic authors as it does to the first historical disciples.[28] But that suits our needs exactly, since it is precisely the shape of faith these figures represent that is the subject of this chapter.

The sense of confidence in the self that typifies this stage of faith comes out in the exchange triggered by the request of James and John for places of privilege. "Grant us to sit, one at your right hand and one at your left, in your glory" (Mark 10:37). The scene is set just prior to the entry into Jerusalem when Jesus' disciples supposed that he would launch the holy war against the Gentiles that would result in superpower status for Israel under the Davidic kingship of Jesus. James and John were asking for cabinet posts in the soon to be formed government. Jesus knew what they wanted, but they did not know what was really in store for them. Jesus foresaw crucifixion and collapse of the movement rather than escalation into military and political triumph. He asked if they were ready to endure what was actually in store for him and for them. "Are you able to drink the cup that I drink, or to be baptized with the baptism with which I am baptized?" The reply of James and John is the motto of the discipleship phase: "We are able" (Mark 10:39). What they were able for was battle and the risk of becoming casualties in the anticipated holy war. They were willing to fight and take their chances. The other disciples felt just as ready and able, as the rest of the conversation shows.

This self-confidence on the part of the disciples is an expression of late Judaism's confidence in the goodness of human nature as God created it. According to this psychology, the natural self is continually under pressure from a good impulse and from a bad impulse, with power to choose between the two. Within this Jewish framework the disciples no doubt viewed the influence of Jesus as informing and strengthening the self to choose the good impulse in service of the vision of establishing the kingdom of God in the style of the golden age of David. They supposed that all that Jesus required of them to share in this dream was to repent, to believe, and to be ready to fight. Jewish confidence in human nature and in Israel's political destiny made them able for this.

Women Who Fit the Mold

Lest one imagine that discipleship macho is a merely male trait, consider the venerable tradition of the all-sufficient woman of faith. Her archetype finds hymnlike expression in the ode to the good wife (Prov. 31:10–31). This woman who "fears the Lord" is "far more precious than jewels" not merely because she is a charming and beautiful companion and mother. There is more. By rising "while it is yet night" and working productively until well after dark ("her lamp does not go out at night") *she* supplies the economic base for the standard of living of her husband and children. Indeed, she earns the status that her husband enjoys—"her husband is known in the gates where he sets among the elders of the land." Max Weber thought he had found the model of the Protestant ethic in Franklin's male figure hammering from five in the morning until eight at night to comfort his creditors.[29] The original is the woman in Proverbs.

She has been there all along, although the control of the literature by males obscures her image. Only occasionally does she come into view, as in the squabble between Martha and Mary (Luke 10:38ff.) or in the story of the Greek woman with enough chutzpah to argue Jesus to a standstill so that her possessed child might be healed (Mark 7:24ff.). She has also been there all along in the attitudes of her offspring. According to Matthew, James and John who gave us the motto for discipleship, "We are able," were put up to their life projects by a believably ambitious mother (Matt. 20:20). And Monica and Suzanna, the mothers of Augustine and Wesley, deserve the credit for the driven quality of the discipleship of their sons.

We live in a time when the drive of discipleship is becoming socially acceptable for women as well as men. We see these superwomen disciples on every hand changing costumes in phone booths, from singles to wives to mothers to graduate students to professionals to staff partners with spouses to singles again. The model from Proverbs is coming into her own.

Discipleship and Ego Strength

The parallel with modern therapeutic assumptions will be obvious. But Paul's term for people who work out of this naturally endowed self was *psychikos,* an adjective built on the root word *psychē,* meaning the soul or the self (I Cor. 2:14). The RSV word for *psychikos* is "unspiritual man," but the footnote alternative, *"natural* man," is more apt. An even more apt translation for our time would be "psychological person." The person who works out of ego strength is the modern-day equivalent of the "soulish" or "psychic" person of Paul's day. These were persons who traced the power of the religious self to the natural vitality all humans share by creation rather than to the special vitality derived from experience of Spirit. Consequently, people in the discipleship phase will desire and profit by counseling and therapy aimed at the strengthening of the self. Pastors of people in this stage will find it important to be able to respond to this desire for the strengthening of the self in the service of the tasks and privileges of the kingdom of God. This reliance on the self to the neglect of the energy of Spirit ranks discipleship as the beginning phase of Christian maturing.

Discipleship and Reparenting

There is, however, a conflict between discipleship's view of self and today's conventional understanding of what constitutes a mature self. Therapy commonly seeks to wean the adult away from dependence on parentlike figures. The mature self is the autonomous self, free to take charge of its own destiny. By contrast, discipleship seeks to reestablish a parenting relationship. This time, however, the parenting figure is no human, but God as heavenly Father. In effect, the disciple is adopted out of his or her natural family into the family of God in order to be resocialized into the values and life-style of this family. Whatever one's natural socialization in childhood, it was at odds with the orientation of the heavenly family and must be redone.

This need for resocialization accounts for Jesus' abrupt way with family ties. He called the original four away from family businesses. James and John left their father, Zebedee, on the shore (Mark 1:16–20). Jesus spurned the summons of his own mother and brothers, explaining to the crowd he was teaching that *they* were his family in the measure that they did the will of God (Mark 3:19b–21, 31–35). He generalized, "If any one comes to me and does not hate his own father and mother and wife and children and brothers and sisters, yes, and even his own *psychē* [as it was formed and continues to be reinforced by worldly influences working through the family], he cannot be my disciple" (Luke 14:26). For those who suppose that the parenting of discipleship will fit smoothly with natural family relationships, Matthew strikes the harshest blow. "Do not think that I have come to bring peace on earth; I have not come to bring peace but a sword. For I have come to set a man against his father, and a daughter against her mother . . . and a man's foes will be those of his own household. He who loves father or mother more than me is not worthy of me; and he who loves son or daughter more than me is not worthy of me" (Matt. 10: 34–37).

These sayings do not mean that Jesus was antifamily. He made marriage and family more secure than any Jewish regulations had (Mark 10:2–16). He confirmed Peter in his family once their home had become the base for his mission (Mark 1:29–34). It was just that in many ways every family delivers us to adulthood at cross purposes with the kingdom of God. Discipleship entails allowing God to parent the adult disciple in ways that compensate for that deforming influence of our natural families. One could summarize Jesus' whole nurture of his disciples as a guiding of them into maturing, as the family of God defines maturing over against the way natural families define it.

My characterization of discipleship as the childhood phase of faith comes from this necessity for all of us in some way to start over again. That is what Jesus prescribed for his grown-up but malformed followers by putting a child in their midst with the comment, "Truly, I say to you, unless you turn and become like children, you will never enter the kingdom of heaven" (Matt. 18:3).

Before considering the content of this new childhood under God's parenting, we need to note the fact that this childhood of faith must have a beginning. The Synoptics picture that beginning in the episode of the call of the four fishermen.

The Call to Discipleship[30]

This beginning is for adults. Discipleship calls for detachment from natural family and preoccupation with work, both of which assume adult status. That is the point of the four fishermen being called away from nets and boats and from the father, Zebedee (Mark 1:16ff.). The disciple is one who subserves his or her workaday life and family commitments to Jesus' mastery. *Detachment* from family and work as the chief expressions of the order of this world, and *attachment* to Jesus as the representative of the order of the kingdom, is the beginning of discipleship. Its contents unfold in Jesus' teaching and example as they come down to us in the stories of his ministry. To adopt as one's own rule of life the new principles of life that Jesus taught and modeled is to launch the reparenting and resocialization that discipleship represents.

Women Disciples

Women as well as men were called to discipleship. Male domination in late Judaism prevented their story from coming to the fore, but women disciples are clearly in evidence. They remain faithful between crucifixion and resurrection, bridging the gap in the process of discipleship nurture left by the failure of male disciples. Women coped better with Jesus' apparent failure. The woman who anointed Jesus for burial earned perpetual fame by accepting a fate for Jesus that no male disciple could stomach (Mark 14:3ff.).

Women had been in the circle of disciples all along, as an occasional saying discloses. "Whoever does the will of God is my brother, and sister, and mother" (Mark 3:35). Mother and sister disciples supported the movement all along (Luke 8:1ff.). They would have made the same moves to disengage from family and work as men. The issue of women leaving work and home to become disciples is behind the complaint of Martha about her disciple sister, Mary (Luke 10:39ff.). No doubt there were disgruntled Marthas all over Galilee who were left with their disciple sisters' share of the housework.

Discipleship in Contrast to Crowd Religion

Adoption of new principles for living distinguishes disciples from the crowd. Members of the crowd sought out Jesus merely for the good he could do them. They never intended to alter their way of life, much less to make Jesus the arbiter of their lives. The story of the ten lepers is a perfect example of the difference between discipleship and crowd religion. Nine who remained with the crowd took their healing and went their merry way. The one who exemplifies discipleship made his healing an occasion for mounting a relationship with God, "praising God with a loud voice," and for a worshipful intimacy with Jesus, "and he fell on his face at Jesus' feet, giving him thanks" (Luke 17:11–19). These characterize discipleship. Parishioners who appear in the sanctuary only on Christmas and Easter are our most obvious "crowd" exemplars today.

The Advantage of Discipleship Over New Creation and Rebirth

The call of the four presents a more realistic picture of the beginning of the Christian life than the metaphors of new creation and rebirth. These tend to promise too much too soon. The call of the four shows not only that disciples must make a conscious and deliberate choice to answer Jesus' call but that a long journey lies ahead of them before the daily leading of Christ their new Master will counter the effects of their former lives. Only this long journey can prepare them to fulfill their destiny to become fishers of others. Discipleship takes account of the long road that leads toward maturing. This relieves the fledgling Christian of the crushing puzzlement and guilt that come when all things turn out not to be immediately and literally new for new creatures in Christ. It allows for the fact that new birth does not simply close off influences of a former life in the days that follow conversion.

The portrayal of discipleship in the Gospels is as accurate in dealing with the end of the road as with its beginning—the story of the faith journey of the first disciples remains unfinished. No Gospel author takes up the task of tracing each of the twelve to the journey's end. That is a parable of the fact that our maturing is never finished. But there is an end to discipleship in the sense of a goal that provides orientation within the always incomplete process of maturing. That goal is given in the metaphor that dominates this book: "I will make you become fishers of men [others]" (Mark 1:17). As disciples we are all destined for mission, so that one of the principal measures of maturing is the extent to which we engage in mission. The prophetic guide to maturing in the Christian life may take the measure of a person's effectiveness by how soon and how well his or her charges become avid, knowledgeable, successful, and peaceful anglers. Isaac Walton, a contemporary of Bunyan, wrote a classic entitled *The Compleat Angler,* which depicts such anglers. Whether or not it was Walton's intention, his book is an apt metaphor of the heart of the clerical calling and of the delightful mood in which it may unfold. Walton's "compleat" angler studies not only how to catch fish but also how to be at peace while doing it. Walton found the joy in the doing as rewarding as the catch. His final admonition, "Be quiet and go a-angling," is worth attending, as is the accompanying quotation from I Thessalonians, "Study to be quiet" (4:11). But much must happen in the new childhood of discipleship before we arrive at such mature poise.

Our Father

The prayer Jesus taught the disciples epitomizes the content of the reworked childhood he prescribed. It amounts to a lesson plan for those responsible for nurturing themselves and others in it. The prayer begins as the petition of a group: "*Our* Father. . . ." God uses the company of disciples as the medium of nurture. The church acts as the family of God to model and reinforce for one another what God is drawing us all toward. Jesus dealt with his disciples as a group, calling four to begin with (Mark 1:16–20). Eventually he selected twelve as a symbol of a new people that this family of disciples was intended to become. Even when they were dispersed for mission purposes, they went two by two. Solo discipleship is an anomaly. Faith matures in company with others. I will not say there is no salvation outside the church. I am prepared to say there is no maturing outside it.

The circle of disciples constituted the new family in which childhood is reworked. In the Synoptic Gospels it is the equivalent of church. That circle came to focus as a table fellowship. That table replaced the table of natural family. The nurturing influence of discipleship was most intense at table with Jesus. The celebration of the Lord's Supper is the sacramental continuation of the disciple circle gathered around its table. Jesus sat at the head of the disciples' table conducting the nurturing process for the invisible parenting God. In the sacrament he continues to preside over our nurture.

"Our *Father*" points to the new parent whose affection, guidance, and careful support shepherds us into new growth. The affection of this father fuels growth and invites our love. As we grow in discipleship, we grow in the degree of our intimacy with the heavenly father until it becomes natural to speak to him with all the familiarity of a child to its daddy. Jesus' "Abba, Father" in the Garden of Gethsemane would be something like "Daddy Dear" in our usage.[31] The loving acceptance of this affectionate intimacy with the single most important other in the universe has power. For those who believe, it overcomes the denigrating and debilitating estimate of ourselves that our natural parenting, our early socialization, and life's daily put-downs have fastened on us.

Here is the true source of the life-giving affirmation we seek from our closest friends and dearest loved ones. They provide what we seek in such imperfect ways that our hearts remain restless until they rest in this father's love.

The cause of liberating women from the oppressive role assignments of our culture complicates discipleship's way of relating to God as a father. Many blame the church's doctrine of the fatherhood of God for the predicament of women in Western culture. This doctrine was used most

recently to reinforce the roles assigned to men and
women in the Victorian family.[32] It is true that doctrines
of the fatherhood of God and the brotherhood of man as
we have inherited them from the nineteenth century do
reflect our culture's way of looking at the masculine role.
That way of looking at men does not do justice to the role
of God grounded in the disciples' prayer in particular and
in the New Testament generally. As the New Testament
presents God in action, God fulfills the best of both masculine and feminine roles in the process of nurturing us toward maturity. These multiple roles attributed to God
lead logically to a doctrine of the Trinity. Within the Trinity the mothering role of Spirit emerges on a par with the
fathering role we are now exploring, and overcomes in
principle the fixing of God as masculine which occurred in
Jewish monotheism.[33] When we come to describe the
phase of the Christian life that I call "transition in Spirit,"
we shall see that God exercises what we call masculine and
feminine roles simultaneously, thus overcoming in eschatological preview the dividing wall of sexuality that so
many now experience. Even in the discipleship phase, the
disciples' prayer counters oppressive associations from
culture.

The petition "Hallowed be thy name" means that this
father is not the same as any other father any of us have
known. An essential meaning of "holy" is separate or special. In its original setting in Judaism this petition
reaffirmed monotheism's main tenet that there is only one
true God. That is being reaffirmed here as disciples confess
that no one else has a comparable claim to our allegiance
or a comparable function as the source of our life. We are
to love *this* one, commit ourselves to *this* one in a way we
have never done with any human being. Holiness means
that this fathering God will never deal with us in quite the
same way any human parent has. We need not fear the
influence of this father, however complicated parenting

has been for us heretofore. To become a child again to this father will lead to our maturing as disciples and not to the childishness of arrested development that natural parenting in some measure imprints upon us all.

Fear of making God masculine will not be the major hindrance for most of us in assuming the new childhood of discipleship. Pride in our grown-up autonomy will be. Adult hubris says we have outgrown the need for parenting with its return to dependence and its reeducation. However grown up we consider ourselves to be, we cannot avoid Jesus' insistence that unless we turn and become as children there is no way for us into the kingdom of God. Too much of what we think we know about life and how it should be lived is foolish and destructive from the perspective of the reign of God. We must allow God to parent us if we are to mature. Christians who think to jump over this phase and rush to bringing in the kingdom in their own adult way inevitably misrepresent that kingdom and bring some counterfeit in its stead.

Thy Kingdom Come

Only reparenting makes it possible to perceive, let alone serve, *God's* kingdom and *God's* will—*"Thy* kingdom come, *thy* will be done." We take these two petitions together because the second is an expansion of the first. It is omitted in Luke and probably was not original in Jesus' teaching. To us the words "kingdom of God" tend to misrepresent the idea that Jesus and the Synoptic writers intended to convey. So much is at stake here because the coming near of the kingdom and its inauguration were the central theme of Jesus' prophecy and teaching. That theme gives discipleship its decisive content.

"Kingdom" implies a particular political institutional form. Most Jews in Jesus' day, including all the original disciples, supposed he was espousing a militant form of what we would now call Zionism, a return to the golden age of David. Most disciples in every era since then have supposed the same. The discipleship phase climaxes with the overcoming of this illusion. We should have known from the start that any political equivalency for the kingdom was out of the question since the distinctive ethics summarized in the Sermon on the Mount make this impossible. Love of neighbor, including love of enemies, is totally incompatible with a political kingdom based on military conquest and maintained by military might.

Jesus' idea of the kingdom of God did not come from Jewish political history but came from the stream of apocalyptic thinking in late Judaism. Daniel is its source rather than the books that record Israel's conquests. The apocalyptic kingdom is a new order which will be given by God from heaven at the coming of the Son of man in clouds (Mark 13:24ff.). We cannot explore here the full meaning of that symbol for the end, but two implications are essential for understanding the parenting process of discipleship. First, although the new order of the kingdom will never be established in this age, it is the order into which disciples are being reparented and resocialized. Jesus came to declare the coming of this new order as God's agenda for humankind. Jesus did not come declaring discipleship for its own sake. Discipleship is intended to serve the new order. This explains the second implication. In the measure that family, work, and traditional institutional religion serve existing worldly orders, they must be left behind. Discipleship calls for detachment from every means that the existing order uses to fasten its values and life patterns on people. That is why the original call to discipleship summoned disciples away from work and home.

God as father parents us into the ethic of the new order of the kingdom. His love is a demanding love. The discipleship stage declares, in the name of Jesus as its authoritative interpreter, that there is no way into the process of maturing in the Christian life without obedient submission to this parenting God. Much of the effort of ministers as prophetic guides at this stage will be devoted to explaining the content of this ethic as the will of the parenting God whose presence comes into our lives and through us into the world by way of this ethic.

Daily Bread

God as the parenting father matches our obedience with provision for all of our needs. We need not limit "bread" to bare necessities, as in a prison diet of bread and water. Jesus' teaching offered more than puritan or monastic asceticism. In response to anxiety about clothes Jesus held up the "lilies of the field" as a lavishly beautiful example of clothing by God that surpasses anything Solomon could have managed at the height of his glory. Beauty is included in daily bread (Matt. 6:25–33). Jesus came eating and drinking in contrast to John the Baptist's "diet for a small planet," opening himself to the charge of being a glutton and a drunkard who "partied" with tax collectors and other sinners (Matt. 11:16–19). Think of how many fine banquets figure in Jesus' teaching metaphors and in the reports of his ministry. Even the bread and wine of the Last Supper were not the whole meal. Dining together stands out as a special feature of Jesus' nurture of his disciples. Luke followed his version of the disciples' prayer with a series of metaphors reinforcing the openhanded provision of God as parenting father (Luke 11:5–13; Matt. 7:7–12).

Christians devoted to the Protestant ethic and used to paying their own way may have difficulty with this "free lunch" policy. It does not intend to detract from the necessity to work, but it does challenge the cause-and-effect relationship between work and provision for material needs. Disciples are being directed to credit God for the fruits of their labor so that his mysterious hand upsets the usual calculus. This means that most of us will get a level of provision far beyond anything we deserve for our work. All of these considerations are aimed at delivering us from the distracting and enslaving anxiety for things that sap life and displace the concerns of discipleship (Matt. 6:33). Only anxiety-free reliance on God's provision for our own needs makes possible the lavish generosity toward God and neighbor that Jesus' teaching mandates (Matt. 5:38–42; Mark 12:41–44).

Conservative Christians represent God more faithfully here than most mainline clergy. Anxiety about career and standard of living automatically overpower church members in the absence of teaching about the fatherly provision of God. For a beginning, most clergy will need to offer what seems to be too much. I think immediately about claims that God provides parking spaces to "revived" believers.[34] When I was a younger theologian and knew better what God would and would not do, I ruled out Yahweh's parking cars. Now I would not put anything past this prodigal God.

I do not mean to suggest that this fatherly God endorses upward mobility as the final consideration in discipleship. That cannot be squared with the saying, "But seek first his kingdom and his righteousness, and all these things shall be yours as well" (Matt. 6:33). Protestants especially misled one another in the Gilded Age that followed the Civil War when they assured themselves that God intended all to "get rich."[35] People who make riches their aim are attempting to create for themselves bogus self-worth and security. In discipleship, worth and security are bestowed as gifts upon all who accept the love of the father of the kingdom and submit to his regulations for life. Jesus taught that having riches makes it more difficult to enter the kingdom (Mark 10:23).

What level of provision should a disciple expect? That cannot be adequately described in the coin of worldly exchange. When Peter asked that question for himself and all disciples, the answer was, "Truly, I say to you, there is no one who has left house or brothers or sisters or mother or father or children or lands, for my sake and for the gospel, who will not receive a hundredfold now in this time" (Mark 10:29–30). The point was that disciples will suffer no sense of loss for having shifted from anxiety about their level of well-being to trust in the support of the parenting God. In fact, we should expect to experience lavish provision, though we must reckon on some changes of taste in the course of our resocialization as disciples.

Forgive Us Our Debts

Having met our anxiety about material well-being, the prayer moves on to the equally important sustenance of preserving us in discipleship in spite of our continuing sins. We never quite slough off the effects of our former socialization, so that the imprint of that conditioning continues to haunt our attempts to act differently. The demons are anxious to fill any space not occupied by the nurture of God (Matt. 12:23ff.). In spite of the rigor of the new regulations, God is not a perfectionist parent, expecting what we cannot deliver. The injunction is to be perfect (Matt. 5:48). But perfection cannot mean what it connotes to us, otherwise the prayer would not provide for daily sinning, nor would there be provision for breaches within the community (Matt. 18:15–20). The theme of the Sermon prior to the saying on perfection has been the contrast between Jesus' rigorous exposition of true righteousness and the Pharisees' relaxing of the commandments.

Matthew's point is that Jesus' ethical teaching takes the exposition of God's will beyond the shortcomings of Pharisaic exposition and on to completion. Disciples must tie their lives to this complete exposition of God's will and in that sense be perfect. "There must be no limits [like the limits being offered by Pharisees], as your heavenly Father's goodness knows no bounds." Breaches of true righteousness with God and within the disciple circle are bound to come. But then they must be repaired immediately, before the sun goes down (Eph. 4:26). And there must be no limit to the number of times forgiveness is offered (Matt. 18:21–22). This continual and immediate process of reconciliation must go on because relationships with God and with other disciples are the vehicles of nurture. Everything depends on keeping them free of obstructions to the flow of the power to mature.

Growing Pains

"Lead us not into temptation" calls attention to the fact that discipleship unfolds toward maturing only by overcoming obstacles to growth. Temptation means "testing" as Jesus was tested by Satan in the wilderness. Just as health in childhood is not the absence of disease, but the overcoming of it with the consequent building up of immunities, so we grow in righteousness as we fall prey to temptation, but build resistance to it in the process. This testing process comes with the territory, since we bring the tapes of our former socialization with us into discipleship. Maturing means suffering through the editing while new tapes of discipleship are being cut to displace the old tapes of crowd religion. The sense of the petition then is, "Do not let me be caught in tests too severe for me to manage in my spiritual infancy, and never, never let me sense that I have been abandoned by you when I fall." You see how the last two fit together. There can be no abandonment by this parenting God who has committed himself along with his whole earthly family to forgiving restoration—whatever may befall.

So much for the prayer as an inventory of important factors in discipleship nurture. The factors of resistance and testing at its end point to the final resistances that must be overcome before the discipleship phase may come to completion. The ultimate resistances to be overcome by reparenting and resocialization are illusions about who Jesus is and what the coming of the kingdom means. They are two sides of the same coin.

Beyond Illusion

Christology and the nature of the kingdom were the issues that caused the original disciples to defect. We can observe a process of dawning appreciation in the case of the first issue. They met Jesus as a prophet announcing the coming kingdom. They followed him initially on that basis. His ministry seemed to be a branch of the movement of the prophet John the Baptist. Then he unfolded a body of teaching about the nature of the kingdom and of life in it. He became their teacher-rabbi. The role of prophet and of teacher were both attested by healings, exorcisms, and nature miracles. At Caesarea Philippi disciples are represented as having put the prophecy and teaching about the kingdom of God together with the miracles and coming to the conclusion the crowd had missed. Jesus was more than a teacher-prophet—he was the Messiah of the coming kingdom. He was not just the herald of the kingdom but the agent through whom God would set it up. So far, so good.

Now the disciples' idea of the kingdom became decisive. Their religious nurture led them to expect the coming kingdom to be a return of the golden age of David. But this time Israel would be upgraded to a superpower that would impose its religion and will upon all the peoples of the earth. The Gentile nations were to become Israel's servants (Isa. 60). The first step in the coming of this kingdom was to be a holy war against Rome led by the messiah in his role as a charismatic warrior. At Caesarea Philippi all this came together. The disciples saw Jesus as this Son of David Messiah. Now they understood why Jesus had gone up to Jerusalem in spite of the resistance to him. He had come to Jerusalem to inaugurate the holy war against Rome in the ancient capital of his people. They began to collect weapons for the fray (Luke 22:36, 38). The disciples did not simply invent this scenario to fulfill some private wish. They had received it as part of their religious training.

Some such illusion about the kingdom and Jesus' role in it seems endemic to discipleship. The church through much of its history has been wedded to some variation of this illusory package. I think immediately of examples such as the church under Constantine; the dream of a holy Roman empire; crusade fever; the political alliances of the Reformation that led to state churches; and, closer to home, the American Protestant project to turn America into the kingdom of God.[36] This misperception of the kingdom of God and of Jesus' role in it is the grand illusion of discipleship.

American disciples still have to move beyond thinking of America as the kingdom of God if they are to complete the work of that phase well enough to move to further maturing. That illusion persists among conservative Christians in their veneration of the economic and political systems of America as adequate vehicles of the kingdom of God. The coming of the kingdom only waits for the imposition of their private morality on the public at large. Current features of that morality include the allocation of national resources to outarm, and, if necessary, outfight the Russians; the return to laissez-faire capitalism in explicit rejection of welfare state compensation for the inequities of that economic system; and a ban on abortion as being a crime equivalent to murder. We saw the movement of this kingdom illusion peak in a coalition of Reagan forces, the Moral Majority, and the right-to-life movement.

Social activist Christians keep a counter hope and companion illusion alive in the form of liberation theology. For them the Vietnam war scuttled the hope of America ever qualifying as the promised land of the kingdom. So, many have shifted their hope to the Third World, where religiopolitical revolutionary movements of the oppressed might provide the occasion for the kingdom's coming there. Jesus is perceived by both types of Christianity as prophetic teacher of both versions of the kingdom. Both are prepared to follow him into holy war.

Transition to the phase of maturing beyond discipleship depends on turning away from these worldly versions of kingdom and messiah. Instead, disciples must settle for an apocalyptic kingdom which can never find adequate political implementation in institutions of this world. This more mature orientation will be content with increasing the level of justice where possible in all human institutions without expecting to transform them into the kingdom of God. Persons may now be recruited to share in advocating and implementing that justice as part of the process of Christian maturing. The final collapse of these illusions about Jesus and the kingdom belongs to the next phase, so we will discuss them in that connection in the next chapter. We need only observe now that discipleship comes to a climax in the shift from hope of our triumph in this world to hope of God's triumph in the next.

Fishers of Others: A Model for Ministry

Meanwhile the parenting God fathers his family toward maturing—illusions and all. As we noted in the call of the four (Mark 1:16–20), the call to discipleship served notice to disciples that they were to become fishers of others. I

shall maintain that this is the ultimate goal of the whole
maturing process within the Christian life. The disciples
were continually reminded of this mandate, for to follow
Jesus was to watch him as he fished for others. All the time
that Jesus was teaching and leading the disciple circle he
was engaged in mission. One cannot avoid the conclusion
that disciples are missioners in training. It was only a matter of maturing and time before they were sent out to
augment Jesus' mission. Eventually Jesus called out twelve
specifically for mission and later sent them out to duplicate
his ministry. The striking thing is that disciples are put into
mission even before they overcome their illusions about
Jesus and the kingdom. Does this suddenly indulgent father put his children in mission at risk of their mixing their
illusions into the action? Apparently so—strange God! The
lesson must be that there is no phase in the Christian life
in which we may plead immaturity in order to be free of
the obligation to participate in mission.

A selection process takes place in connection with the
call to augment Jesus' ministry. Only some of the company of disciples get to duplicate the public ministry of
Jesus—preaching to the crowds, teaching disciple groups
that respond, dealing with people one by one as they
come forward, and healing as they go. The analogy to the
professional ministry is obvious. Most Protestant theologies of ministry interpret ordination as the call to preach,
teach, pastor, and administer the Sacraments to a largely
passive assembly of hearers in obvious imitation of the
model we see Jesus display in the Gospels. The Reformation definition of the church as present wherever the
Word is rightly preached and the Sacraments rightly administered duplicates this picture of ministry. Only one
person on the scene holds a pole. The rest presumably
are fish to be caught. This picture in the Gospels of Jesus
as model for ordained ministry is so powerful that it has
seduced the church in general and clergy in particular

into adopting it as the complete picture of ministry. This particular picture is most appropriate to the discipleship phase of Christian maturing. It misrepresents the rest of the New Testament's doctrine whereby ministry belongs to the whole church without the distinction we make between laity and clergy.[37] This other picture of ministry emerged in the so-called theologies of the ministries of the laity.

After a flurry of such theologies not much has changed in the churches. We may begin to benefit from these seemingly competing doctrines of ministry only when we begin to appreciate that each correlates with a particular phase of maturing in the Christian life. The picture of ministry we see displayed at eleven o'clock on Sunday morning in the average local church is one most appropriate to the disciple, or childhood, phase of faith. As clergy and laity in a particular congregation move beyond that phase, the eleven o'clock service will need to change to meet the new situation. Other forms of gathering and other configurations of ministry will need to emerge. The eleven-o'clock Sunday-morning ministry will always continue at least as fishing ground, launching pad, and seedbed, out of which subsequent phases of growth in Christian life and ministry emerge. How to match forms of ministry with phases of maturing will be the subject of the final chapter. But there are particular implications of the discipleship phase for clergy development that are best attended while this phase is freshly before us.

Discipleship Phase for Clergy

If the experience of a few clergy is typical, many of us spend half our careers under the spell of the illusions of the discipleship phase. For clergy these illusions are variations of the basic illusions about Christ and kingdom we traced in discipleship. If we substitute career for kingdom and

minister for the Christ figure, the implications for maturing begin to unfold.

Most contemporary Christians have no eschatology
comparable in scope to the one we saw in the Gospels.
Apart from hope for personal immortality, we make little
use of the images of the return of Christ, the end of this
world, and a great judgment. There is perhaps a vague
hangover of the traditional confidence that America is so
special it will become the scene of the final unfolding of
the kingdom of God. In the absence of confidence in the
biblical images for the end, we tend to be at the mercy of
the apocalyptic image of nuclear holocaust. This seems to
be the only image for the end that has much power in
church or culture today.

This substitution of an image of nuclear holocaust for the
coming of Christ is a parable of what happens to Christians
when they cease to believe in their own eschatological
heritage. The culture supplies its own images for the end
when we default by ceasing to believe in biblical images
of God's triumph at the end. Clerical careers tend to fall
prey to a similar process.

Most of us respond to a call to ministry with particular,
beloved and effective clergypersons in mind. As we observe their ministry we see God challenging human lives
with the transforming power of the gospel. Since we long
for such challenge and transformation, we suppose the
people in those congregations do also. We respond whole-
heartedly and we suppose those congregations are doing
the same. Our call often comes as we observe some model
clergy figures who are at their best speaking in public.
There is little real appreciation among admirers of how
seriously hearers are actually taking these persons they
admire. Candidates for ministry vastly overrate the influence their favorite clergy are having. Consequently, prospective ministers are able to sustain their dream of ministry until their first call or appointment to parish leadership

after graduation from seminary and full ordination. Then the reality of the profession tumbles in on them.

The reality is that the vast majority of persons in a typical congregation do not want themselves or their world to be transformed by the gospel. Instead, they want the minister to help them make life easier to manage while they and their world stay the same in every important respect. The gospel says that we and the world orders in which we live must be changed to enjoy its blessings. The good news most people want to hear is that we can be blessed without anything changing. For most beginning clergy that is a wrenching revelation. Our road takes a turn toward Jerusalem. The congregation's view of ministry is very different from ours. We come wishing to be change agents in the name of the gospel of Jesus Christ. That is the meaning of ministry to which we responded and which our theological education has reinforced. Their view is that ministry is to support the status quo. Which view will prevail? Here we finally touch bottom. When we realistically assess the actual situation of the minister in a local congregation, we are forced to conclude that the people in the congregation have more power to change us than we have to change them. How we respond to this turn of events determines the shape of our ministries for the next ten to fifteen years.

Most of us have little choice but to accommodate to the congregation's view. No one has warned us that this is what the ministry is really like. Nor has our training equipped us to deal with the reality when it comes out.

At this point the eschatology of the culture fills the vacuum our preparation for ministry has left. We are in desperate need of an eschatology of some kind, for our world threatens to come to an end. But the end is not yet. There is an unconfessed eschatology at hand within the churches. It is no less real or powerful because it remains unstated. Dean Hoge has exposed the current eschatology

of Protestants in the institutional church.[38] Underneath
the professing of most church people that they are pursuing traditional Christian values and churchly mission goals
there lies a more fundamental commitment to what Hoge
calls the big three. Typically, church members, clergy and
lay, are most deeply committed to family, career, and
standard of living. Whenever we are challenged by competing values, these three prevail.

Caught in the backwash of broken dreams of being
change agents, young clergy shift toward pursuit of career
as an alternative future. Advocacy of personal and social
transformation fades as a major preoccupation of ministry.
Career becomes the dominant eschatology for the profession. An unspoken contract gets struck. If we exert ourselves to provide what the institutional church wants at
local and denominational levels, we will be rewarded with
career advancement. From this point on, our ministries
tend to be driven by pursuit of career rather than by
passion for change.

To retain or recover our original dream in the face of
career eschatology we will need to take certain steps. Discipleship nurture for clergy will mean clustering with
other clergy who are resisting this takeover of the eschatology of career. This disciple circle will need to find
together the means of grace to purge its members of domination by the big three until some more faithful form of
ministry emerges. I am confident that can happen—but
not unless clergy arrange for themselves a nurturing process similar to the one we have described in the discipleship phase.

I hope I have not drawn too dark a picture of the first
and formative years as a pastoral leader. For many readers
what I have described will not fit their experience. All my
reading and observation tells me that it is an accurate
picture of what happens to most of us. It is nothing any of
us ought to feel ashamed of. The culture and the institu-

tion to which we belong prescribe it for us. It is merely the churchly version of what happens to most adult males in our culture. I doubt there is much we can do about it until it happens to us, given our lack of warning and preparation. What matters is that we take vigorous action when we come to realize what is happening.

If this description of the predicament of the minister does not strike a chord of recognition now, eventually it will. Perhaps we may be fifteen to twenty years into ministry. That is how long it usually takes for career advancement to reach its peak. That point in our careers is like the experience of the first disciples when their career dreams vanished at the arrest of Jesus and the prospect of his execution. They had done what Jesus asked in the hope of a career in the coming kingdom. From their point of view it seemed that Jesus had defaulted on their deal. They forsook him and fled.

We experience a similar sense of betrayal. We have contracted with the institutional church for career advancement. Then the institution fails to keep its part of the bargain. Sometime in our forties or fifties we realize that we will rise no higher. There will be no larger or more challenging parishes to lead. How we respond to this jolt to our hopes will determine our path of maturing from then on. The description of the next phase of faith journey deals with this response. If we respond appropriately, *this time in our careers may usher in a golden era* of usefulness and satisfaction.

CHAPTER 3
TRANSITION IN SPIRIT

The Cross as the End of an Illusion

From the beginning, Jesus, the teacher of discipleship, had been implicitly challenging the illusion of a nationalist, ethnocentric kingdom coupled with a militant messiah. The challenge intensified after the disciples developed to the point of recognizing him as the Messiah, and not merely the prophet of crowd perception. The challenge became explicit when in response to their confession Jesus began to predict his suffering, his rejection by the nation's leaders, and his ensuing death. Peter, speaking for all the disciples, could not, of course, square this outcome with his illusion of militant triumph. So Jesus rebuked him with the same language he had used to exorcise the demons from the man possessed and began to draw the implications for discipleship: "If any would come after me, let them deny themselves and take up their cross and follow me." (See Mark 8:34.)

The self to be denied was the self that had projected its childish, tribal dreams onto the parenting God of the kingdom. The cross stands athwart the path of the journey of faith, barring the way to further development until we come to terms with our illusions about what God was up to in Jesus of Nazareth. Sooner or later, disciples must face

72

the fact that a crucified Christ cannot be made to be the patron of the misfit dreams of discipleship.

The cross of Jesus is the perfect squelch to the illusion of worldly triumph. Everything about the manner of his death militated against this illusion. When he was arrested, he refused to fight. His disciples had armed themselves. One actually struck what he supposed was the first blow for freedom by cutting off the ear of the slave of the high priest. Though Jesus was arraigned before the Romans as a dangerous subversive, everyone knew better. The disciples knew better after the fiasco of an unresisting arrest. Then the crowd knew better too and asked instead for Barabbas, a certified freedom fighter. The manner of Jesus' death did not make sense from the perspective of the illusion of Davidic triumphalism. So those who chose to continue with this crucified Christ needed to make new sense of the selves they had formed around this illusion.

It does not matter which side of the cross you may be on chronologically. The need for the cross to reform the self of the Christian persists long after the event is literally behind us. In Mark's day the triumphalist Davidic dream had reared its head again in the form of the holy war of the Jews against the Romans (A.D. 66–70). Followers of Jesus were being recruited to participate in that war and were responding. The cross was not seen as a barrier to joining up. Zealot Christians probably interpreted Jesus' death as one more glorious instance in a long line of martyrs in the cause of national liberation. Palestinian Christians were being asked to follow this example. Mark made sure that this interpretation of Jesus' death was struck down by highlighting the incongruity between the public charge of revolutionary subversion and the whole manner of Jesus' own conduct. Mark carefully edited the story of the passion to end the same illusion in his generation that had plagued disciples in Jesus' day. The same task of setting cross over against illusion must be repeated in every

generation and within every Christian self bent on maturing.

As we have suggested already, the cross challenges the
favorite forms of the classic illusion in our generation.
Immature evangelical disciples seek national triumph
through a moral majority at home and military superiority
abroad. Immature social activist disciples seek kingdom
triumph by pluralistic tolerance at home and wars of national liberation abroad. Selves formed in the service of
these illusions must suffer a psychic death of disillusion-
ment before new selves may be formed in the service of
the fresh realities God holds out to us in the phase of the
Christian life that follows. But the first grand dreams of
discipleship die hard.

The Trauma of Gethsemane

There seems to be no way around some trauma in the
process of the psychic death and dying that accompanies
the dispelling of illusion. In the Garden of Gethsemane,
Jesus modeled the transition in the self that the cross eventually calls for in us all. His invitation to the disciples to
accompany him in the original experience is our invitation
to follow as well.

The story clearly displays trauma. The pathos of dying
surrounded Jesus' plea to be relieved of the burden of his
dreadful fate. The mood of mourning is caught in the
words, "My soul is very sorrowful, even to death" (Mark
14:33–34). An ancient reading in Luke heightened the
trauma: "And being in an agony he prayed more ear-
nestly; and his sweat became like great drops of blood
falling down upon the ground" (Luke 22:44). In Matthew,
"he fell on his face and prayed." What is there about this
transition that fells us so? The prayer itself tells.

"Abba, Father"—here is the confidence and security of
the intimacy built through many experiences of answers

to the disciples' prayer. "All things are possible to thee"—here is the childlike illusion that no serious hitch need ever develop in the lives of the children of an omnipotent parent. So far it is all in keeping with the childhood phase. Then comes the glimmer of a new perception of God and self—"yet not what I will, but what thou wilt." At this point the self breaks the chrysalis of childhood. It entertains the idea that God has not been seeking in God's Messiah what we have wished. God's will and our wills have been on divergent courses.

The Last Supper

The Last Supper, preceding Gethsemane, launched the transition beyond discipleship illusion. It offered the initial clue to the meaning of Jesus' failure to triumph. By identifying the broken loaf and poured-out wine with his body and blood, he announced that these symbols referred to his impending death. The meaning of the death was that it was "for many," and Matthew adds, "for the forgiveness of sins" (Mark 14:24; Matt. 26:28). When the disciples first joined him, they supposed they had ceased to be sinners, since by following Jesus they had repented and believed as both John's and Jesus' teachings had prescribed. Only now it turns out that in their believing in the coming kingdom they had not ceased to be sinners but had become a new kind of sinner—the kind that substitutes one's own worldly, status-seeking projects for the kingdom of God, while claiming sanction for them from the God of that kingdom. It is sobering to come to realize that Christ died precisely for religious people actively committed to the coming of the kingdom. But it was a kingdom born of illusion, not God's kingdom.

It is precisely while we are being so utterly religious that we need forgiveness most. No wonder the disciples' prayer calls for daily forgiveness. What did the first disciples think the Supper meant as they celebrated it before its postdiscipleship meaning began to dawn? We perceive the Sacraments according to the phase we are in when we celebrate. For the first disciples and all disciples since, the Supper was and is an anticipatory victory banquet. We lift the wine in a stirring toast to the victorious kingdom: "Truly, I say to you, I shall not drink again of the fruit of the vine until that day when I drink it new in the kingdom of God" (Mark 14:25). "Cheers!" But when we become willing to hear, the cup word and bread word invite us to see our illusions for what they are and to leave them behind. In a highly artful way Mark shows us this "leaving behind."

The Young Man as Archetype of Transition

*See
Harrington,
Mark,
pp 226-27
& 244-45*

Mark never showed the name disciples as making the transition he was prescribing—presumably because the militant Christians of his day were using the Twelve as patrons to justify their refusal to move on to greater maturing. So Mark supplied a no-name figure to show the way. It was done so subtly that the lesson is usually overlooked.

A young man makes two appearances in Mark, one at the scene of the arrest, where all the disciples forsake Jesus and flee (Mark 14:50; Matt. 26:56) except for this young man. He "followed him, with nothing but a linen cloth about his body; and they seized him, but he left the linen cloth and ran away naked" (Mark 14:51–52). The second appearance of the young man (the same Greek word is used) is at the empty tomb. "And entering the tomb, they [the women who have come to complete the burial] saw a young man sitting on the right side, dressed in a white robe; and they were amazed" (Mark 16:5). The young man announces the resurrection and tells the women to deliver a message to the disciples and to Peter. We miss the continuity between the two appearances partly because Matthew turned the young man into an angel and Luke made him into two men, but mainly because we do not realize that Mark is inviting us to a transition beyond discipleship.

Apart from the lesson of the young man, disciples in Mark go from misunderstanding to betrayal, with no subsequent rehabilitation. Missing this lesson of the young man is what makes the book of Mark so unsatisfying. Mark meant for the double appearance of the young man to repair the gap created by the collapse of discipleship. His lost shirt represents the illusion that must be left behind, the nakedness represents the trauma involved, and the white robe points to the new realization beyond illusion. The young man models for us what the relentlessly militant disciples could not.

There is comfort in Mark's having to resort to the young man. If a wing of the church in his day was using the original Twelve to prolong their discipleship phase, we must not be too hard on ourselves or our parishioners if we discover ourselves caught in a similar resistance to maturing. There is indeed a long and venerable tradition that argues for arresting development in the phase of discipleship.

Collapse from Within

For the original disciples and for disciples in Mark's day, discipleship collapsed from without. Jesus refused to start a holy war. A generation later his countrymen tried it, but it ended in a fiasco that nearly obliterated Palestinian Judaism. Periodically the message of the cross comes to us from without whenever our holy war plans come to naught. For most generations the course of events does not force an end to discipleship's dreams. Nevertheless, if God is good to us and we avail ourselves of the means of grace, discipleship eventually collapses from within.

There is simply not enough psychic return in keeping the
ethic of discipleship to make up for the loss of worldly
return that ethic entails. Virtue is not its own reward.
Loving your enemies puts you at a distinct disadvantage
in a competitive climate where they are likely to sock it
to you if you turn the other cheek. To forgive *and forget*
is asking to be taken advantage of a second time!

The resources of the self are no match for storms of
anger and resentment at the loss of worldly advantage, let
alone the lust and craving that regularly flash across the
horizon of the interior life. With time the point emerges
at which our plans for self-gratification are hopelessly at
cross-purposes with the commands of the Jesus we have
sworn to follow. Then Paul's description of the journey of
faith on the verge of transition to Spirit becomes our story.
"So I find it to be a law that when I want to do right, evil
lies close at hand. For I delight in the law of God [repre-
sented now by the commandments of discipleship], in my
inmost self, but I see in my members another law at war
with the law of my mind and making me captive to the law
of sin which dwells in my members. Wretched man that
I am! Who will deliver me from this body of death?" (Rom.
7:21–24).

It is not just the failure of the self in the face of an ethic
now experienced as too demanding that pushes us on to
some new phase. There is a restlessness with religion itself.
The whole round of observances and obligations comes to
be felt as a burden in an already burdened life.

My own childhood was set in a congregation of Scottish
Covenanters full of just such righteous but weary saints.
The heavy righteousness was epitomized in the stiff faces
of the choir that sang of that righteousness. A saint has
been defined as someone who makes goodness seem at-
tractive. These saints made goodness seem merely obliga-
tory. They were bound and determined to be good even
if it killed them. It is this weariness with well-doing that

finally puts a permanent cloud cover over discipleship. John Wesley expressed the feeling of this period of the faith journey when he confessed, "I dragged on heavily."

We now have a word for this crisis when it is connected with work among clergy and other helping professionals —burnout. Those who do not go on to some new phase of maturing may simply revert to their predisciple life-styles. "Simon Peter said to them, 'I am going fishing.' They said to him, 'We will go with you.' " Until we transit this dead end, we are more battered by sin and baffled by our inability to deal with it than at any former time in our lives. Wesley found that those "who were thoroughly bruised by sin willingly heard and received . . . [the good news of a further phase of faith] gladly."

Failing some transition to greater maturing, weary saints must lead double lives—a righteous life to ease the conscience and a fun life to make the righteous one bearable. With time, this back-and-forth existence is likely to lead to cynicism and emotional withdrawal from professional tasks.

Perhaps the most common refuge today in this wasteland period of the journey of faith, for lay and clergy alike, is the "affair."[39] When God and all the commitments we have made in God's name seem to be receding from us, the closeness of a fresh sexual partner partly fills the space that distance from God and covenant partners leaves. The diversion enables us to avoid, for a time, the mounting pressure upon us to make the transition to greater spiritual maturing.

The good news that there is more to the Christian life than this often leads to what seems like a conversion experience. John Wesley returned from Georgia a failure as clergyperson, suitor, and Christian. Peter Böhler persuaded him, from Scripture and the experience of acquaintances, that there was more to the faith journey than he yet knew. In that hope Wesley went one night to Aldersgate Street, where his heart was strangely warmed as Luther's "Preface to Romans" was being read. That experience launched Wesley's ministry as the instrument of the evangelical awakening in England and eventual founder of Methodism. It was fitting that Wesley should catch this experience through Luther, for, as a weary monk, Luther had had that same kind of experience in the tower.

In the full flush of the positive side of this transition experience a person supposes that he or she is now really Christian for the first time. That was Wesley's judgment when he recorded the Aldersgate experience. In his subsequent maturing he revised that judgment.[40] I am suggesting that the so-called conversion experiences of Wesley and Luther and many others are really transition experiences.

see n. 40, p. 190

Resurrection Realization

Mark's young man shows us the first step on the positive side of the transition we are describing. In the slough of despond that had enveloped everyone when discipleship collapsed, he had the grace to remember that Jesus had promised something more. On the merest hunch that there might be more, the young man went out to the cemetery to see if perchance Jesus had escaped being entombed by the collapse of the disciples' dreams. The young man was the first to discover that the tomb was empty. Mark judged that no appearance of the risen Christ was necessary for the faith journey to resume—just the empty tomb. Mark offered the empty tomb as a symbol of the faith fact, that when our dreams die, when the life of faith collapses under the weight of illusion, Christ is not consigned to the tomb, nor does the whole structure of faith collapse. Instead, Christ waits beyond the wreckage of our first attempts to follow him to assure us that the most exciting phase of the journey of faith is about to begin. This realization was given to the young man for us all. To come to the point where you realize there is more is to begin to believe in the resurrection. Without that realization no amount of mouthing of Easter confessions counts. To believe in the resurrection is to believe the promise that the risen Christ waits for you beyond discipleship.

To be sure, there were appearances of the risen Lord to the first disciples. Mark's account without those appearances means that for all subsequent generations, what matters is not appearances but the promise. Resurrection promises an experience of the risen Christ in a completely different mode from the one familiar to discipleship. Mark only hints at the new mode with the Baptist's promise that Jesus "will baptize you with the Holy Spirit" (Mark 1:8). The major contribution of the Fourth Gospel and of Luke is that each undertook to display this new mode of faith that succeeds the "following" of discipleship.

John's Mode of the Presence

John related his new mode of Christ's presence directly to the problem posed by the empty tomb. That problem is where and how we may experience the risen Christ when he is no longer visible out there in front of us leading as he did in the days of his flesh. "Blessed are those who have not seen [the risen Lord in objective form] and yet believe" (John 20:29) is precisely to the point. By the time that benediction was pronounced, the solution had been given.

In the farewell discourse, beginning at John 13:31 and ending with ch. 17, John's Jesus forced the problem of the mode of his continuing presence on the disciples before it had become an issue for them. In a variety of ways he warned them of his coming absence: "You will seek me; . . . so now I say to you 'Where I am going you cannot come' " (13:33); "I go to prepare a place for you" (14:2); "I will not leave you desolate" (v. 18); "You heard me say to you 'I go away' " (v. 28); "But now I am going to him who sent me" (16:5); "It is to your advantage that I go away" (v. 6); "A little while, and you will see me no more" (v. 16); "I am leaving the world and going to the Father" (v. 28); "And now I am no more in the world" (17:11). The warning of his impending absence triggered the central question for the experience of post-resurrection faith and for the transition we are discovering: "Lord, how is it that you will manifest yourself to us?" (14:22). John's answer is his doctrine of the Paraclete. The Paraclete is the substitute or alternate mode of divine presence filling the void left by Jesus' going away: "The Father . . . will give you *another* Counselor [Paraclete] to be with you for ever" (14:16); "The Counselor [Paraclete] . . . whom the Father will send in my name . . . will teach you all things [just as Jesus had been teaching them everything], and bring to your remembrance all that I have said to you" (v. 26); "When the Counselor [Paraclete] comes, . . . he will bear witness to me" (15:26).

So concentrated is this alternate presence on the things of Jesus that it seems almost to be another Jesus: "The Counselor [Paraclete], . . . whom the Father will send in my name, he will . . . bring to your remembrance all that I have said to you. . . . Peace I leave with you" (14:26–27); and "He will take what is mine and declare it to you" (16:14). Indeed, to live in this presence is the same as to abide in the risen Jesus (15:1–11).

Although functioning as an alter Jesus, the Counselor (Paraclete) is actually the Holy Spirit (14:17, 26). This clarifies the situation. The divine presence that replaces Jesus is another person of the Godhead. The transition from discipleship to life in the Spirit introduces a trinitarian note into the journey of faith. We shall return to trinitarian consciousness as a mark of this transition. The point at hand is that the Spirit's presence as Counselor (Paraclete) solves the problem to faith of the vacancy left by the departure of the Jesus who had led in discipleship, and shifts the life of faith into another mode than "following."

The problem, as John put it, recalls the bereavement at Gethsemane and the heaviness that comes as the disciple-ship phase wears out. The disciples were troubled and afraid (14:1, 27); they felt desolate (v. 18); they were in-clined to defect from faith altogether (16:1); sorrow had filled their hearts (vs. 6, 20, 22); they would weep and lament; and they would scatter in unbelief (v. 32).

The realization that the problem has been overcome allows John, in contrast to the Synoptic presentation, to concentrate on the positive effects of the transition, namely: life (14:6), rejoicing (16:22; 17:13), joy (16:20), full-ness of joy (15:11; 16:24; 17:13), and peace (14:27; 16:33); coupled with the confidence that nothing that happens in the world can any longer take that joy and peace away (16:22, 33). Now it is possible to continue to believe (14:29; 16:1). *In the light of this shift of the focus of faith from Jesus to Spirit in the farewell discourse, we see that the full force of the good news of John's Gospel is experienced not at entrance into discipleship but at transition to life in the Spirit.*

The experience of this joy and peace in believing is available only after resurrection realization has dawned upon disciples, for it is the risen Christ who breathes the Spirit on his followers, not the Jesus of the ministry and of discipleship. With that breathing and receiving of the Holy Spirit, discipleship ends and a new phase of faith begins. John portrays it as an advanced phase with special advantages (16:7): new access to truth (vs. 13, 15); height-ened intimacy with the Father and with Jesus (14:20, 23; 15:1–11; 16:23, 26; 17:3, 6–8, 21–26); and the prospect of greater effectiveness in mission (14:12, 13, 14; 15:5, 7, 16; 16:8–11).

It is to this experience of transition that John's famous metaphor of the new birth (3:3–8) applies and not to the entrance into discipleship. New birth is the work of the Spirit, and the Spirit was not yet bestowed during the discipleship phase. Even if Nicodemus had understood the need for another birth, he would have had to wait for it until after the resurrection. When the American tradition of evangelism insists on using this metaphor for the entrance to faith, it tends to misrepresent that entrance, to malign people who have already begun the journey of faith as disciples, and to deprive the church of the challenge to mature which the original thrust of the metaphor offers. The greatest blessing of the Christian life comes not at the beginning but in the experience of this transition to life in the Spirit.

The Shift of Locus in Faith Experience

Periodically in the life of the church some author recovers this revolutionary insight and makes it available to others. For example, Henry Scougal's *The Life of God in the Soul of Man* performed that service for George Whitefield. John Wesley appreciated its point as well and issued an abridged version of the book in 1742. The message continued to be so constantly discovered that a reprint was issued every three years in the eighteenth century. Scougal's thesis: "True religion is a union of the soul with God, a real participation of the divine nature, the very image of God drawn upon the soul," is a fair summary of the shift of locus in faith experience that comes with transition to life in the Spirit.[41]

We saw how Mark hinted at this shift by relocating the divine presence from the Galilee of Jesus' ministry to the Galilee of the landscape of faith. John described the shift explicitly. In the time of discipleship John's Jesus says, the Spirit "dwells *with you*," as the power leading Jesus in his ministry. With transition the Spirit *"will be in you"* (John 14:17). The Counselor (Paraclete) fills the vacuum left when Jesus rose to the Father. The limited energy of a self misguided by illusion drove the life of discipleship. Now the life of faith is driven by the unlimited energy of the Holy Spirit. The raising of consciousness that accompanies this shift of focus is the difference between living as an alienated slave who moves in sheer obedience to commands that a slave has no way of understanding, and living as a friend who works out of understanding sympathy with another friend who explains everything as they go. The slave brings no heart to the task. The friend works from the heart. "No longer do I call you servants, for the servant does not know what the master is doing; but I have called you friends, for all that I have heard from my Father I have made known to you" (15:15).

This change in the quality of relationship inaugurates an intimacy that removes all distance between the believer and God: "We [the Father and Jesus] will come to [believers in transition] and make our home with [them]" (14:23; 17:22). This presence of the Spirit within each believer bringing with it mystical union with the Father and the Son empowers the believer beyond anything that was possible before: "Truly, truly, I say to you, any who believe in me [and this new mode of God's presence] will also do the works that I do; and greater works than these will they do, because I go to the Father" (14:12). This intense intimacy makes possible not only new levels of effectiveness in mission but new levels of holiness in the believer's life. "Sanctify them in the truth" (17:17), which is to say, disciples may now become holy by means of the truth of this new intimacy with divine life to a degree never possible before. The contrast in mood between discipleship faith as a burden to be borne and transition faith which bears one up by the grace of the Comforter-Paraclete justifies the drama in the metaphor of rebirth.

The gift of the Spirit provides the second chance that the collapse of discipleship requires. "I have said all this to you to keep you from falling away" (16:1). What keeps the believer from falling out of faith is the relocation of divine presence as Spirit within rather than as historical Jesus out in front. When John portrayed the resurrected Jesus breathing the Spirit upon the defected disciples, he reenacted creation. As Yahweh breathed Spirit into the molded but lifeless body of Adam (Gen. 2:7), the risen Christ breathes life into the bodies discipleship has molded.

The Situation for the Doctrine of the Paraclete

About A.D. 85, Judaism declared Christians heretics and took steps to exclude them from the synagogue. This is obviously the bind that Johannine disciples were in (John 9:22; 16:2; 19:38). Under pressure of excommunication some were falling away. The doctrine of the coming of the Spirit presented in the farewell discourse was designed to keep this defection from becoming final (16:1). According to the editor of John 21, the original disciples, representing Johannine Christians, had already "gone fishing," that is, they had dropped out of mission rather than face the pressure of persecution. Just as the arrest and threat of death at the hands of Jewish authorities had brought the discipleship to an end originally, so arrest and threat of death (16:2) were bringing discipleship within the Johannine community to an end. To stay in the journey of faith would require an infusion of new life to transform faith in the face of persecution. The breathing of the Spirit on the disciples by the risen Christ symbolized that revitalizing infusion. The obvious allusion to the act of creating Adam by the breath of God recalls the root meaning of Spirit as breath of life.[42] The parallel with Ezekiel's vision of the resuscitation of the dry bones is especially apt (Ezek. 37:5,

9–10). John's community needed to come back to life by means of the Spirit, just as Israel had needed to in Ezekiel's day.

The metaphor of paraclete gave the doctrine of Spirit the shape it needed to meet the judicial process of expulsion, judgment, and persecution. "Paraclete" is a forensic term for the lawyer or counselor who acts for a client on trial.[43] Accordingly, the Paraclete was the one who stood up in Jewish court for the disciples under accusation and threat of judgment. Jesus had modeled this counselor role in the case of the man cured of congenital blindness (John 9). The cured man stood up for Jesus under examination by the Jews and was cast out for wanting to become a disciple (vs. 27, 34). Then Jesus sought him out, welcomed him to discipleship and rebuked the Pharisees, hence the aptness of the Paraclete as "another" or second counselor (14:16). The courtroom context for the metaphor is confirmed by John's picture of the Paraclete turning the tables on the world as it brings Johannine Christians to trial, accusing and convicting those who had brought the charges in the first place (16:8–11) just as Jesus had done for the. cured blind man. Jesus' action on behalf of the blind man showed the Paraclete not merely in a defensive role but taking the initiative to support and vindicate Jesus' own, whatever their fate in court. Thus the idea of Paraclete includes mediator, intercessor, and helper, as well as advocate or counselor.[44] Provision of this supporting, empowering role by the Paraclete enabled the Johannine community to continue to engage in its mission to Judaism even after expulsion.

Luke's Version of Transition to Spirit

Luke too developed his form of transition to Spirit with reference to Judaism and mission. The book of Acts shows representative missioners of the early church beginning

with Stephen and ending with Paul. Each took the gospel
first to the synagogue, experienced rejection, and then
moved out to the Gentiles. In Acts the Jews continually
blocked the missionary activity of the church by attempting to take its representatives into custody, whereupon
the Roman government would step in to offer protection.
The church's strategy was to claim legitimacy as Jews before Rome in spite of rejection by Jewish edict. This strategy worked until the end of Domitian's reign, when, in
A.D. 96, legal status as Jews was withdrawn from the
church. In the period between 85 and 96, Luke argued
that the church was the true Israel because it was observant (this was expressed decisively by the edict of the Council of Jerusalem), but even more because it had received
the eschatological promise of the Spirit (Joel 2:28–32; Acts
2:17–21).

To define the church as eschatological Israel and not
merely as observant Israel, Luke transformed Pentecost,
the Jewish festival to commemorate the giving of the Law,
into a commemoration of the giving of the Spirit. When
Luke argued for the true Israel as the eschatological community of the Spirit, he declared in effect that discipleship
was a preliminary and incomplete expression of faith. During the ministry, Jesus, not the disciples, had the Spirit,
and therefore disciples only qualified as the true Israel
after they received the Spirit at Pentecost (Luke 4:16ff.;
Isa. 61:1–2).

By Luke's time the political illusion of discipleship characteristic of Mark's time had been dispelled by Roman
victory in A.D. 70. The illusion that clouded discipleship in
Luke's day was an apocalyptic one, namely, that since the
time was so short and the kingdom so near, the eschatological community of the Spirit did not need to take bodily
existence and historical tasks seriously. In particular, disciples felt free of the obligation to continue in mission. Luke
countered withdrawal from bodily existence with the bla-

tantly bodily quality of Jesus' resurrection—"See my hands and my feet, that it is I myself; handle me, and see; for a spirit has not flesh and bones as you see that I have" (Luke 24:39). Apocalyptic withdrawal was corrected by rejecting immediate expectation of the end (21:8b; Acts 1:6–7) and by substituting mission in the power of the Spirit for idle curiosity as to the time of the end (Acts 1:7–8).

In the light of this situation Luke made three major points in his portrayal of Pentecost. First, the Spirit was really given to all the followers of Jesus, marking them as the true, eschatological Israel. Any followers of Jesus or of John the Baptist who had not received the Spirit were still living the obsolete life of the old Israel which had only the Law and the historical Jesus, but not the eschatological gift of Spirit. Secondly, although the Spirit was indeed an eschatological gift, Spirit was only available on condition that the new Israel reject preoccupying concern for the end and commit itself to mission (Acts 1:8).

Thirdly, Luke meant the tongues of Pentecost to be real foreign languages rather than the ecstatic speech of glossolalia. The commitment to mission is the point of the real foreign languages at Pentecost when bystanders "from every nation under heaven" heard the people speaking in different languages, telling in their own tongue "the mighty works of God" (Acts 2:5–6, 11). Luke's presentation of speaking in tongues as speaking real foreign languages confirmed the missionary thrust of life in the Spirit. What world mission needs is foreign languages, not ecstatic babble. It also guarded against the unearthly spirituality of withdrawal from common life that glossolalia tended to induce. Most probably the presentation of real Berlitz type languages and a flesh-and-bones, hungry and lunching risen Christ were both directed against the temptation to equate the life of faith with esoteric experiences in withdrawal from the real world.

Luke took such care in explaining the manner and content of the speaking "in other tongues" that it is hard to resist the conclusion that he was fending off a Corinthian-like version of that experience. Jesus in the incident in the synagogue at Nazareth modeled what Luke intended speaking in the Spirit to mean. Following the lesson from Isaiah that the Spirit had anointed him to act in the role of a prophet to "preach good news" (Luke 4:18; Isa. 61:1), Jesus sat down to do just that in the plain language of the synagogue. In volume two Luke used Joel to explain the anointing with Spirit to the same purpose. Joel specified that the Spirit was given for prophecy: "I will pour out my Spirit; and they shall prophesy" (Acts 2:18; Joel 2:28). That is exactly what each recipient of the Spirit does at Pentecost: "telling [in plain language] . . . the mighty works of God" (Acts 2:4) by recounting "the sending and exaltation of Jesus."[45] Peter's address filled out the meaning. Both the rank and file of Christians at Pentecost and Peter, the apostle, illustrate the eschatological gift of the Spirit as the plain-language preaching that Joel had foretold.

Luke's lesson that the Spirit is a gift for proclamation is reinforced by the other two occasions in Acts where speaking in tongues is reported. At Acts 10:46, Luke used a variation of the same expressions found in 2:11 alongside "speaking in tongues," so that prophesying in a foreign language is most probably meant again.[46] Peter's companions from Joppa in a multilingual society would presumably have recognized other languages than their own. It is clear in the explanatory comment "and extolling God" that what was being said was understandable. Only plain language would have let them know that God was being praised. Luke used the same word to introduce the sublimely clear Magnificat of Mary's praise (Luke 1:46).

There is no doubt what Luke meant at Acts 19:6: "The Holy Spirit came on them; and they spoke with tongues *and prophesied.*" Here the pattern prescribed in Joel and explained at Pentecost reoccurs. "And prophesied" stands in apposition with "spoke with tongues," explaining the contents of the speaking. Luke had found an ingenious way to follow Paul's advice to the Corinthians of permitting speaking in tongues but urging pursuit of the higher gift of prophecy by simply combining the two into a single gift!

I have taken such care to define what this one striking manifestation of Spirit was in Luke's church in order to show that Luke's portrayal of transition to Spirit does not support the interpretation imposed upon him by Pentecostalism and by some charismatics. The book of Acts does not recognize glossolalia as an indispensable mark of spiritual maturing. Quite the opposite—Pentecost meant that transition to Spirit calls the maturing disciple to serve the mission of the church to the whole world by proclamation in all its languages. Luke meant to displace the unintelligible speaking we know from Corinth.

There are no New Testament texts that justify Pentecostal or charismatic gatherings where many people speak in tongues without interpretation. Luke meant to discourage such by his portrayal of Pentecost. In this he carried out the spirit of Paul's regulations whereby at most two or three speak in tongues and then only when someone interprets for each (I Cor. 14:27–28). Neither Luke's record of Pentecost nor any other New Testament text justifies mass glossolalia. Such practice comes from the spirit of worldly culture, not from the Holy Spirit.

There were other aspects of the experience of transition to Spirit that Luke wished to emphasize. The experience of the Spirit is the climactic aim of all prayer (Luke 11:13; Acts 1:14). Experience of Spirit binds believers together as a community of love (Acts 2:43–47). Experience of Spirit provides such transforming intimacy with God in Christ that seeing the glory of God, the believer is effective in witness and unshakable in persecution (7:54–60).[47] The

Spirit accounts for making joy and praise the dominant moods of the Christian life (2:47; 3:8–9; 4:21; 5:41; 13:52).

But one cannot do justice to post-Pentecostal life in Luke's church by listing its features. The experience of that church under the power and leading of the Spirit is actually an interconnected whole in which repentance, faith, prayer, baptism, the Lord's Supper, communal meals, laying on of hands, interpreting Scripture, speaking in foreign languages for proclamation, guidance in mission by the Spirit, and shared life in the church each has a place. I have space to pick out only what applies particularly to a scheme of the faith journey.

As a transition beyond the conditions of discipleship the most important thing to observe is how the Spirit makes up for the loss of the role that Jesus played in the life of the disciples. To emphasize the transition to a new situation Luke alone gives us the forty-day interval between resurrection and ascension. That, coupled with the scene of ascension, again only in Luke, dramatized the absence of Jesus and the need for an alternate form of divine presence for the life of faith. By virtue of Pentecost, the Spirit now led and empowered believers in the same way that Jesus had led and empowered them by his presence (Luke 4:14, 18, 19). In the time of the Spirit, disciples who formerly followed Jesus' leading are led by the Spirit instead.

Discipleship, as a following of Jesus moving on ahead, no longer fit the circumstances. The Spirit, not Jesus, now points the way, not from up ahead, but by prompting from within. Luke continued to use the disciple metaphor. For the purposes of our sketch of the Christian life, however, a shift in terminology helps us note the need to change our orientation to God in order to tap the new mode of divine presence. Luke's continuing use of "disciple" for the post-Pentecost Christian, of course, justifies that same usage today. Those who prefer Luke's scheme will need to take Lucan pains to show the difference between life ante-Pentecost and post-Pentecost.

In Luke, the church's special term for Christianity is "the Way" (Acts 9:2; 19:9; 22:4; 24:22). While Luke does use the expressions "way of God" and "way of the Lord" (18:25–26), the prominence he gives to the role of the Spirit would suggest strongly that "way of the Spirit" or "the journey of faith led by the Spirit" would be the most appropriate paraphrases. As commentators frequently suggest, the book would be aptly named "The Acts of the Holy Spirit." At crucial times on the unfolding way of the early church, the Spirit calls the turn (8:29; 11:12; 13:2; 16:6, 7; 19:21).

These dramatic leadings at forks in "the Way" imply that all along the church was being led and empowered by the Spirit whether that was reported explicitly or not. Jesus' baptism in Spirit as he began his Galilean ministry provided the underlying assumption of his whole ministry. Occasionally the empowering Spirit surfaced, as in the challenge to his exorcisms, when refusing to acknowledge the power of the Spirit in them amounts to the unforgivable sin.

The Spirit of Mission

Luke's major contribution to our understanding of transition into life in the Spirit is to put that experience in service of mission. The point of the coming of the Spirit into the church's life is not to provide some rush of feeling of fulfillment, but to launch believers into a particular Way of life. The Way is what occupies the attention, not the emotional overtones. Above all, where the Way leads is what counts. Luke said, "Look to the ends of the earth." Discipleship amounted to a pilgrimage for the grail of upward mobility. With that preoccupation disposed of, the faith journey turns into a missionary journey.

Pentecost certainly was a dramatic experience for its participants, but to center one's attention on the experience per se would be to substitute another distracting illusion for the ones given up in discipleship. Transition in Spirit draws us into a way of life, not just into one more conversionlike experience. The risk in any discussion of experience of Spirit is the tendency to seek the experience for its own sake. I can only grieve that most exegetes still represent Luke as continuing to foster ecstasy as *the* mark of the Spirit's coming when Luke substituted foreign languages for "tongues" to dispel that distraction. A survey of Spirit experiences in the New Testament forces me to conclude that "speaking in tongues" in a Corinthian sense had not worn well in the church since Paul, and that Luke offered the next generation, and offers ours, a compelling alternative. Transition to life in the Spirit is transition to a life empowered for missionary engagement—never to a life preoccupied with religious experiences. As we shall see, Paul, who endorsed Corinthian tongue-speaking, had a way of setting the context that put tongues in the service of mission. In fact, Paul is our best New Testament witness to the inner quality of life in the Spirit. What John promised and hinted at in the farewell discourse and what Luke described as a somewhat impersonal power in Acts, Paul described in terms of intimate personal relationship.

The source of Luke's doctrine of Spirit was the Old Testament idea of Spirit as special additional equipment for carrying out particular tasks. Luke's major variation on that idea was that all believers now have this special equipment, not just heroic figures with special commissions. Luke thought of that special equipment as a supplement to faith. In Acts it was possible to believe and not have the Spirit.

Spirit Intimacy in Paul

Nothing epitomized Paul's view of life in the Spirit as new intimacy with God as much as did prayer in the Spirit. Its most dramatic form was speaking in tongues. In Pauline congregations a more accurate expression would be *"praying* in tongues," for this is what was taking place (I Cor. 14:13–16). The Spirit supplies a heavenly prayer language, different from any of the languages available in the world. Even the person who is praying may not understand. In a deeply moving and faith-confirming way God assures the praying charismatic not only that the prayer is being heard but that it is being supplied as well. As a consequence the believer feels caught up into the awesome intimacy that flows eternally within the Trinity themselves. The praise, thanksgiving, and adoration being offered and received are too deep for ordinary words. This being caught up into intratriune intimacy is calculated to wean us away from preoccupation with self in order to allow Christ to occupy our consciousness.

Pentecostals and charismatics tend to overplay Spirit-generated prayer in the form of mysterious language. Paul offered Spirit-generated prayer in other forms as well. One form is simply nonverbal. The Spirit intercedes for us in sighs too deep for words (Rom. 8:26), what we now call meditative or silent prayer. The other form is in the ordinary language of intimacy, such as, "Abba! Father!" (Rom. 8:15).

In every case, with or without intelligible language, every form of prayer in the Spirit begins from the basic premises that we are "led by the Spirit of God" (Rom. 8:14) and that "we do not know how to pray as we ought" (Rom. 8:26). How different this is from the disciples' prayer in which we are taught to bring any petition we wish (Mark 11:24; Matt. 7:7–11). The puzzle of this carte blanche prayer is solved by the missing element of the Spirit's role in generating prayer. John's version of that same saying included the role of Spirit. "If you abide in me [in the Spirit], and my words abide in you [supplied by the Spirit], ask whatever you will, and it shall be done for you" (John 15:7). All open invitations to prayer in the Gospels assume the conditions John states. Silent prayer, constant prayer (I Thess. 5:17), and intercessory prayer all begin to make sense when we come to realize that the Spirit catches the believer up into a cycle of divine overture and response which the Spirit herself generates.[48] This experience of Spirit in prayer is the ultimate expression of the relocation of divine life within the believer that is such a prominent feature of the life in Spirit phase.

Holy Spirit—The Feminine Side of God

The feminine side of God finally comes to the fore in the experience of Spirit. Intimacy requires an "other" to complete the relationship or else intimacy collapses into sheer subjectivity. The form of this divine other does not derive from the Spirit. The Spirit is in herself formless. In the experience of Spirit intimacy, the form is Christ's. Paul says, "I am again in travail until Christ be formed in you!" (Gal. 4:19), not until the *Spirit* be formed in you. The Spirit is content to be completely self-effacing, so that the face we behold in the process of our transformation is the face of the Christ, not of the Spirit. Therefore in our sanctification we experience the Spirit as "Spirit of the Lord"; indeed in such face-to-face encounter "the Lord is the Spirit" (II Cor. 3:15–18). This self-effacing deference displays the metasexual role of "she" which I suggest we associate with Spirit.

This self-effacing and intensely intimate quality of life in the Spirit calls for associating the feminine aspect of Trinity with Spirit. The more we learn about the maturing adult, the more we come to realize that all of us, whether physically male or female, have the capacity to exercise both masculine and feminine traits. Men and women who open themselves to a total experience of personhood are on their way to greater maturity. Openness to this trans-sexual, bipolar exploration of life means freedom from the rigid truncation of life that the cultural definition of sexual roles lays upon us all. Jürgen Moltmann has pointed out that one amazing ramification of Christianity's peculiar doctrine of the Trinity is the way it transcends the patriarchalism implicit in Jewish monotheism as well as the matriarchalism implicit in pagan pantheism.[49] Using sexual terms in a metasexual rather than a literal, genital, and bodily sense, the feminine dimension of personality refers to the receptive, passive, self-effacing, care-receiving capacity in us all that contrasts with the initiating, aggressive, self-assertive, self-sufficient traits we associate with the masculine dimension. In conventional parenting, from which our paradigm arises, the female supports programs, designs, and goals for family life set by male initiative. The mother supports and nourishes children unconditionally, while the father conditions his support on performance. The traits our culture assigns to the female side of life have bodily correlations in the acts of fertilization, childbearing, and nursing.

In the discipleship period God is experienced mainly as male. Favor is conditioned on obedience. This call for obedience in turn generates a masculinelike initiative taking and self-reliance on the part of the believer. But that is not the whole story. Even within discipleship, the limits of conventional masculinity in God are threatened, anticipating a shift. The father in the parable of the prodigal son acted more like a mother in receiving back so wayward a child unconditionally. Remember how the father in the parable "had compassion and ran and embraced him and kissed" the son before there was any chance for him to test the son for signs of repentance.

Too little notice has been taken of this unconventional father of Jesus' teaching, but Moltmann finds one excellent example. The Council of Toledo of 675 attributed a feminine side to God. In explaining the procession of the Son from the Father both as a begetting and a birth, it included a motherly role for the Father. "It must be held that the Son was created, neither out of nothingness nor yet out of any substance, but that He was begotten or born out of the Father's womb, that is, out of his very essense."[50] This expansion of our appreciation of God to include feminine dimensions, even when God is called "Father," points to a comparable expansion of the dimensions of the life of the believer opened to Spirit.

Holy Spirit—The Feminine Side of the Life of Faith

The receiving of the Holy Spirit adds the feminine dimension to the life of faith that discipleship overlooks. Until the Spirit's coming, discipleship has been predominantly a masculine response. In it we create a life of faith to offer to God as our achievement. We take the initiative to satisfy the conditions placed upon us, however costly. We generate images of a conquering kingdom with a masterful messiah to match. In short, disciples act out masculine traits. The transition to Spirit finds disciples, worn out by these masculine efforts, ready to receive the life we had hoped to generate ourselves. The idea of the Council of Toledo has a counterpart for faith experience. The Spirit provides a nesting place in each believer for the growth of the divine life. Transition to life in the Spirit is a kind of faith pregnancy in the course of which Christ is formed in each of us (Gal. 4:19). The righteousness *we* had hoped to achieve as disciples grows and kicks within us. We stop generating long-range plans and strategies for God and the kingdom. We relinquish the grand strategy to God and content ourselves with knowing the course one day at a time. Not sure where the course leads, we settle for love and patience over knowledge. Satisfied with a life of adoring gratitude to God for this intimacy, we permit ourselves to enjoy the company along the Way. In short, we act out feminine traits. This does not mean that we drop the masculine side of the life of faith. From now on it will not be either masculine or feminine but will be both. In the world to which we are propelled in mission we will seem predominantly masculine, but in our relationship with God we will seem predominantly feminine. Because the coming of the Spirit opens up this feminine side of the life of faith, I have spoken of Spirit as "she." The Spirit is feminine in the Hebrew Old Testament. She became neuter in the shift to the Greek of the New Testament. Reflection on the effects of Spirit on the life of faith helps us to undo this linguistic neutering. We need to honor the Spirit's deferring to Christ in order to come to the heart of the experience of transition to Spirit.

The Face of the Crucified One

The face of the Christ who is formed in us in the Spirit womb is the face of the crucified One. That face transforms us as we come to realize that the act of crucifixion was not just a judgment upon discipleship illusions, but a declaration of God's love as well. As disciples we may have confessed this by mouth before but never savored it in our hearts. Why? Until we experience the collapse of religious self-confidence and detect the alienation from God's true purposes brought on by macho religious consciousness, we have no real sense of the deep tragedy to which our religiosity contributes. Until we experience some degree of our own dereliction from the will of God even while we repeat petitions such as "Thy will be done," we cannot sympa-

thize with Jesus' own cry of dereliction. Without ever
knowing quite why it works this way, we only know that
we, who ought to be abandoned by God for our perverse
misreading of God's reign, never will be because Jesus was
abandoned in our stead. So we find that just when we have
forfeited all claim to acceptance, the eternally feminine
God has found a way to accept us nevertheless.

The dawning realization of so great a love begins to
effect the lifelong process of transformation that is life in
the Spirit. It was Wesley's basking in the new light of this
feminine love of God and sensing its promise of continuing
transformation that warmed his heart at Aldersgate. But
one has to have experienced the demolition of the masculine house of self, built on the sands of an achieved righteousness, before there is any possibility in one's own life
of the atonement becoming relevant, let alone transforming. The fiasco of Wesley's ministry in Georgia, the collapse of his courtship, and the fear of death on the voyage
home all conspired to unlock the feminine receptivity
masked by Wesley, the disciplined masculine and accom-
plished athlete of the religious life. All those turned him
feminine and receptive to life in the Spirit.

The thing that makes the transition to life in the Spirit
so difficult to entertain is the religious resistance to it that
we have built into our lives all during the discipleship
period. We ground the illusions that flaw our lives with
elaborate biblical theological rationalizations. Consequently we live out these illusions with a good conscience.
Should someone challenge these illusions, we imagine ourselves in the role of a heroic confessor, another Luther
crying out, "Here I stand. I can, God helping me, do no
other," when all the while God is trying to help us get
beyond the position we so heroically espouse. For most of
us it takes a collapse something like Wesley's to undermine our carefully constructed theological rationalizations. Seriously religious nuts are the toughest ones to

crack, therefore the trauma of Gethsemane, the bitter tears of Peter, and the leveling of Paul into the dust of the road to Damascus. When we finally do crack, we are ready for one last feminine form of dependence.

Led by the Spirit

Stripped of religious rationalization and accomplishments, we are ready for the first time to be led in life by the Spirit rather than continuing to lead our own lives. The Spirit's leading introduced the Christian phase of redemptive history. Immediately upon Jesus' baptism with the Holy Spirit, the first and archetypical action of the Spirit was to lead him: "Then Jesus was led up by the Spirit into the wilderness" (Matt. 4:1; cf. Luke 4:1; Mark 1:12— "The Spirit . . . drove him . . . "). For the sake of the narrative, Jesus becomes the active agent after the temptation—"Jesus came into Galilee" (Mark), "withdrew into Galilee" (Matthew), or "returned in the power of the Spirit into Galilee" (Luke). But as Luke's "in the power of the Spirit" suggests, the continuing assumption of all the Evangelists was that Jesus was being led by the Spirit throughout the ministry.

Paul carried this crucial assumption about life in the Spirit over from Jesus to all believers: "For all who are led by the Spirit of God are sons of God" (Rom. 8:14; cf. Gal. 5:18).[51] We have already noted this leading at the crucial turning points of the church's mission in Acts. The Spirit's leading works through prayer in the Spirit. The context is individual, "Abba"-intimacy and churchly community in ultimate commitment to mission. Under these conditions God gives direction for mission. In this phase of the faith journey one adds an expectation of personal, direct communication from God to the disciple practice of hearing and obeying the Jesus tradition. A major task of this phase is to grow accustomed to what Thomas Kelly called "inner

guidance and whispered promptings of encouragement
from the Center of our life."[52] *The Imitation of Christ*
called it "the pulse of the divine whisper."

Risky as subjective leading may seem to the disciple
accustomed to the more objective orientation of Jesus'
teaching and example, this is the way maturing lies. Until
we overcome our resistance to it and practice it to the
point of being comfortably confident of the Spirit's guidance, our spiritual lives stay on "hold." We gain confidence
in our reading of the promptings of the Spirit as we risk
"practicing the presence of God."[53] A certain amount of
trial and error is inevitable. It helps to avoid injury to
ourselves and to others if we practice with a safety harness
tended by a spiritual friend or director over the safety net
of the church's counsel and tradition. People who wish to
perform the high-flying routines of life in the Spirit without such aids reveal that they are still in the grip of self-
reliant individualism so characteristic of discipleship.

We are talking about what is sometimes called the mystical dimension of the faith journey. It is more apt to speak
of the dimension of intimacy. Mysticism connotes religious
eccentricity. Within the tradition of biblical and
trinitarian Christianity it would be eccentric not to come
to be on intimate terms with God. That is what the gospel
eventually invites and requires. Only within this intimacy
does the life of faith receive the emotional energy and
concrete guidance required to move beyond childhood to
maturing. Without this intimacy and guidance, not only
will our spiritual growth stop but sooner or later, reli-
giously speaking, we will display the bizarre behavior of
the emotionally deprived. The spiritually deprived missionary becomes a stunt man or woman bent on getting
God and neighbor's attention by outrageous gestures of sin
or sanctity, deep plunges of doubt, or Icarian flights of
faith. In terms of classic temptations it is the dream of hang
gliding from the pinnacle of the Temple.

Summary

Transition to life in the Spirit entails three major moves. First, it entails an acute consciousness of the worldly illusion that dominated our discipleship and a turning from the religious selves constructed upon them. This is modeled in Gethsemane. Secondly, it entails acceptance of the forgiveness made possible in the crucifixion. The offer of forgiveness through the cross is accepted in partaking of the Lord's Supper in the light of the guarantee of the resurrection. Thirdly, the departure of the risen Christ opens the way to fresh intimacy through the gift of the Spirit. In this new intimacy the support and direction that mission requires become the common everyday experience of one who practices the presence of God.

To make the transition, some ruling misconception about the religious life must be given up. In Mark it was that the kingdom would come as a political takeover through holy war, with the spoils of victory as reward. In Matthew it was the hope that by keeping the will of God in the scaled-down version being codified by the Pharisaic court at Jamnia one could earn eternal life. In Luke it was the temptation to withdraw from mission to the world on the basis of a docetic Christology and calculation of an early restoration of the kingdom to the new Israel in an apocalyptic act. In John it was fear of rejection and reprisal by Judaism for continuing to adapt the Christian tradition to Hellenistic pluralism for missionary purposes.

I have argued that it is important to distinguish the phase of life in the Spirit from the phase of discipleship even though we are used to equating discipleship with the whole of the Christian life. Discipleship as I am defining it is that phase of the Christian life when Christ is experienced primarily as a figure of the past who continues among us in his teachings and example. The essential mode of contact with him is to remember. God, the Father, in this mode of piety is at an austere distance "in heaven," although at work in the world in mysterious providential ways. The particulars of that providence remain shrouded in mystery. Just as mysteriously, this remote God intervenes in life to answer prayers of petition that do sustain our lives in the particulars of bread and forgiveness in the measure we trust him and repent of our sins. We experience God the Father remote in spatial terms just as we experience Jesus remote in time. The genius of the transition I am pointing to is that both God as Father and Jesus as Son now draw near and by taking up residence within us become involved in prompting, teaching, and empowering us from the center of our lives. God, as Father and Son, experienced as intimately engaged for missionary ends is the experience of God as Holy Spirit.

The experience of Spirit as I have portrayed it differs from the version offered in Pentecostalism and the charismatic movement. I have appended an extended note on tongues for those whose ministry calls for care of charismatics and Pentecostals. (See Appendix I.)

The Continuation of Discipleship

Phase theory dictates that no previous phase is ever left completely behind as we move to more mature phases. The new phase includes all that was valid in the previous phase and depends on it as the ground of every advance the new phase presents. Two elements in discipleship that become obsolete are concentration on the historical Jesus as Messiah and the illusion of upward mobility which clouds the kingdom his Messiahship serves. Once the historical Jesus is displaced by the risen Christ encountering us in experience of Holy Spirit and the kingdom is disengaged from every worldly dream, the whole body of the

Synoptic tradition takes on transformed significance. The Spirit loosens that tradition from its confinement to the first century and applies it to the fresh circumstances of our day. The lessons of the Lord's Prayer become fresh realities for us as we cease to strive to make them come true by our own efforts and accept them as gifts of Christ in the Spirit instead. For example, we continue to be forgiven daily but with less lingering regret that we had not done better. We continue to ask for daily bread but with less anxiety about how much we must do first before accepting any "free lunch." We hallow God's name by confusing it less with human parenting figures who conditioned their care for us on the standing we had earned by our performance. In short, we are enabled by the Spirit to penetrate the cover of the historical Jesus, disclosing the splendid, transforming face of the crucified and risen Christ. The Synoptic tradition continues to ground the life of Christians in every subsequent phase as the risen Christ shares the Spirit with former followers who may now have the same energy they observed in Jesus but could not yet share.

Implications of Transition to Spirit for Clergy

I think it fair to say that the theological education of the vast majority of clergy will have prepared them to recognize some familiar doctrinal themes in the above exposition but little that is familiar to their experience. We are all victims of the way theology has been done in the West since the split with Eastern Orthodoxy. When they chose to put the experience of Spirit at the center of their theological task, we chose to put rational, doctrinal reflection at the center instead. The result has been massive neglect of the experience of the Holy Spirit in the training of Western theologians, Catholic and Protestant. Protestants have suffered most since we have no lively tradition of spiritual theology. The only comparable attention to experience in Protestant seminaries has been clinical pastoral education, but it sets experience in the context of a psychology of the self rather than in the context of a theology of the Holy Spirit. Protestants are just now beginning to catch up to Catholics by adding seminary courses in spiritual formation and by mounting continuing education programs for preparation of spiritual directors. These efforts are too late or too unavailable for most of us. Clergy will have to band together to teach themselves. The times call for a massive effort of remedial theological education for the clergy of the West. Only by coming to terms with an experience of Spirit of their own do clergy have a ghost of a chance to fulfill their calling. Every layer of the New Testament testifies that the ministry of the church is conducted by the Holy Spirit. Clergy may have a share in that ministry in the measure that we fall in with the movement of the Spirit. Until we do, the ministry of clergy and laity alike will mainly be spinning of institutional wheels.

We saw at the end of Chapter 2 how the forsaking of the eschatology of career is the beginning of readiness for ministry in the Spirit. To begin there means readiness to accept a call or appointment to a particular post solely on the basis of the missionary task it represents under the prompting of the Spirit. To be open for this means to have learned the lesson of discipleship to the point that God must be trusted to provide support for the standard of living appropriate to our families. It seems we cannot break with one of Hoge's big three without jettisoning the other two. Probably that will mean staying longer in small parishes that worship in buildings with low steeples. We shall agree to career moves only with the sure confidence that they are the leading of the Holy Spirit. For most of us that will take much greater sensitivity to the prompting of the Spirit than we now possess. Assuming a first degree from the school of discipleship, we shall now have to add continuing education in the school of the Spirit.

I continued my education by reading Douglas V. Steere's *Prayer and Worship* in connection with the rich and convenient sampling of devotional classics found in a pack of pamphlets issued by the Upper Room called Living Selections from Devotional Classics. From them I have been led to works of Thomas Kelly, John Woolman, and William Temple. You will find your own way from there. It is catching! In the vein of spiritual direction, Kenneth Leech's *Soul Friend* sets the stage. I plan next to go on to Baron Friedrich von Hügel's classic, *The Mystical Element of Religion.* Morton Kelsey's *The Other Side of Silence* serves notice that we shall have to imagine a spectrum of approaches to Spirit sensitivity to allow for varieties of temperament and personality.

This is merely a hint of the record of my prompting toward ministry in Spirit. Dip anywhere into the vast but neglected library of devotional literature and the way opens of itself. I suspect we shall be building shelves in our studies to accommodate a devotional collection nearly equal to the rational collection we were trained to accumulate.

To this budding understanding of experience of the Holy Spirit we shall need to add a laboratory component. This calls for a radical reordering of our lives. To go to school with the Spirit we must set aside twenty or thirty minutes of prime time morning and/or evening to put ourselves at the disposal of the Spirit in prayer. Without this provision for basking in the Spirit's presence, we shall never cultivate the sensitivity to the Spirit's prompting that authentic ministry requires. In the 1960s my interest in Zen finally led to the same conclusion. After several years of approaching Zen as a philosophy to be studied, I chanced upon a master whose observation almost induced satori. The insight was: Zen is sitting. For those of us in the West who have approached Christianity as if it were a

philosophical system to be learned it is high time we came
to a similar conclusion. Christianity is praying. For us to
get on with our spiritual maturing, faith must become a
waiting and listening alertly for the breeze of the Spirit.
We shall become fully Christian in the measure we fall in
with the movement of the ongoing ministry of the Holy
Spirit. The first two phases of the Christian life suggest an
agenda for this praying.

Step one is to consider the lilies of the field. The free-
floating and unresolved anxieties connected with family,
career, and standard of living must all be identified and
eased from our shoulders on to those of Christ. We labor
and are heavy laden under the yoke of these anxieties until
Christ relieves us and we find his yoke easy and his burden
light. There is no shirking of our responsibility here. We
will be directed to work for which there is compensation.
Resolution of anxiety comes when we attend to the work
and trust God for the level of compensation.

Attending to that work is the second step. Now we discover or reaffirm the focus of our calling by retracing the
Damascus road of our own call to a particular ministry.
Krister Stendahl is quite right in *Paul Among Jews and
Gentiles.* Paul's Damascus road experience was a call to a
particular ministry rather than a conversion. Its major
effect was that Paul came to realize that, from his mother's
womb, his destiny was the mission to the Gentiles—a good
thing too, for he was a "bust" among the Jews. Clarity
about who our "Gentiles" are would deliver us from the
clerical equivalent of the "Peter principle." Without this
clear targeting by the Spirit, we find ourselves accepting
appointments or calls among people with whom we are
not particularly comfortable, for whom we do not particularly care, and to whom we do not have anything special
to say. Paul loved his Gentiles more than livelihood, went
to any lengths to serve them, and found his message for
them constantly expanding and deepening in its apprecia-

tion of what God had done for their salvation in Christ. As
a result of listening for this focus we shall either relocate
or settle in contentedly where we are to discover over
time what the Spirit is up to among our people.

Most of us are too busy inventing ministry and fretting
over its outcome to realize that the Spirit has been concerned for our people and conducting a ministry among
them long before we arrived and will continue to do so
long after we have gone. The name of the game is not
thinking up ministry where we are but listening for what
the Spirit has in mind. We are to look to the mind of Christ
rather than the mind-set of clergy preoccupied with ministry to an institution.

Ultimately the ministry belongs to the laity. The site of
their ministry is not the institution but the house where
they live, the place where they work, and the political
communities represented on the ballots in their voting
booths. The Spirit is encouraging them to minister there.
Our task as clergy is to see how the Spirit is imagining
using the institution to make their ministries beyond the
institution more effective. Once we get in the spirit of that
ministry I am confident that the Spirit will rise to become
a trade wind of strategy, tactics, and programs filling the
sails of all our ministries.

There is one final agenda item for our praying. It does
not really fit within an order of prayer, since it hangs like
a cloud over the whole order until it gets some measure
of resolution. It will continue to be a constant presence
even then. I am speaking of the chronic weakness or failing we all discover in ourselves after wrestling with God
in our gardens of Gethsemane. The discipleship phase collapses largely because of this weakness. We must identify
it and learn to live with it in the Spirit in order to mature
into useful vessels of graceful ministry. If you are unaware
of your weakness, you are not yet into the transition we are
discussing. No one wrestles all night with God without

limping in the morning and ever after. The weakness may
be associated with failings or strengths. Paul had both
kinds. It is revealing that he picked "coveting" as his example in Romans 7. Did he covet the authority of recognized apostles like Peter? But Christ delivered him from
that failing, according to Romans 8. That was not his
chronic weakness. His chronic weakness was one that
played off of his strength. He was chronically disposed to
exalt himself because of the privileged revelations he received. Paul never outgrew this tendency to pride and
arrogance. Accordingly, he was given a chronic illness to
keep him reminded of his chronic disposition to hubris.
"To keep me from being too elated by the abundance of
revelations, a thorn was given me in the flesh, a messenger
of Satan, to harass me, to keep me from being too elated"
(II Cor. 12:7).

A Catholic priest charged with the care of clergy once
generalized that in his experience the two major pitfalls
among his charges were "Punch and Judy." I find their
appeal ecumenical. For Protestant clergy I would add ca-
reerism and the star consciousness that waits in the wings
to seize preachers with good communication skills.

There is really no need for a catalog of clerical vices. All
experienced clergy will know only too well the Achilles
tendon that snapped, thus hobbling effective ministry just
when they were hitting their stride. For long-standing
weaknesses of which you are acutely aware, two responses
will be appropriate. First, give up imagining that you will
ever be cured of this weakness so that it will no longer dog
your life. Second, settle down to live with your weakness
the way an alcoholic does with alcoholism. Expect to need
strengthening a day at a time for the rest of your life.
People who live in the Spirit live with the consciousness
of weakness. The comfort is that when we are weak, then
and only then are we strong. Actually, it is a relief to be
rid of the consciousness of strength.

Chronic weakness is likely to draw long-standing guilt in its train. If we are unable to throw off the pall of this guilt using the ordinary means of grace, it is time to seek out a spiritual director. He or she must be someone who, hearing the full confession of our weakness and accepting it, is likely to become the vehicle for our hearing Christ say, "Neither do I condemn you; go, and do not sin again." With guilt behind us and confidence in the power of the Spirit of Christ to sustain us in the future, we have set our feet on the path that leads to maturing in church and in mission—the third and culminating phase of the Christian life.

CHAPTER 4
MATURING
IN CHURCH AND MISSION

PART I. MATURING IN CHURCH

Humbling and Reaffirmation

The collapse of discipleship in transition to Spirit is an astonishing experience. All the confidence in the dedicated self that was building during discipleship comes undone. In the denial of that confident self, all self-confidence evaporates. Imagine with what groans of regret the original disciples kept recalling their abject failure to keep their pledge to remain faithful to Jesus no matter what (Mark 14:27–31). They had intended to do so well but had done so poorly. They knew they were forgiven, but Judas remained a reminder of the despair they all had felt. In the throes of recall all must have thought themselves chief among sinners.

The leveling of Paul in the dust of the Damascus road and the days of hopelessness that followed symbolize the humiliation that is the background against which maturing must unfold. Given captivity to the conditioning influences of the world upon even the most religious of us, there is no going on to a life of maturing without the trauma of humiliation. Luke was making this point when he revised the story of the call of the four fishermen to an encounter that dropped Peter to his knees confessing: " 'Depart from me, for I am a sinful man, O Lord.' For he was astonished, . . . and so also were James and John, sons of Zebedee, who were partners with Simon" (Luke 5: 8–10).

The astonished humiliation that comes with the realization of the depths of our defection shakes disciples to the core, so that we rise with joy at forgiveness and new hope, but unsteadily. Jacob is the perfect metaphor for this precarious state—blessed, yes, but halt from then on. "The sun rose upon him as he passed Penuel, limping because of his thigh" (Gen. 32:31). Whether we think of ourselves as newborn or a new creation of the Spirit, both metaphors point to a shaky, vulnerable stretch of life ahead.[54]

Luther, following Augustine, thought of this as a time of convalescence; so did Wesley. Two weeks after Aldersgate, he wrote, "Yet I felt a kind of soreness in my heart, so that I found my wound was not yet fully healed."[55] To steady up on the new course of life Wesley took a moratorium from ministry for a visit with the Moravians in Germany. He was seeking healing sanctuary. This vulnerability of the budding devotee of Spirit Luther spoke of as "the misery of infirmity" which is "only gradually healed by grace in the inn where Christ the Good Samaritan has placed us." The name of this inn is the church. We are healed in company with others.

The Church as the Body

The recognition of the church as the inn where one goes to receive healing strength for growth in maturing is the first step toward that growth. Paul's doctrine of the church as the body is most apt at this phase, since it depends on life in the Spirit. The church is that place on earth where intimacy with the risen Lord continues in a healing bond that equips us for mission in a new key. The power of this intimacy is the Holy Spirit. The distinctive mark of this idea of the church is the assumption that all its members are aware of their endowment with the Spirit.[56] The church as the body of Christ is that group which is conscious of having made the transition to life in the Spirit and who covenant together to live out the implications of that supreme fact of their lives.

At this point it is helpful to make a distinction. The followers of Jesus began their journey of faith without access to the Holy Spirit for themselves. The Spirit had been given to Jesus only, but after the resurrection the Spirit became available for all as a new component of the life of faith. For us today who begin the journey of faith post-Pentecost, access to the Spirit has been granted at baptism. The gift of the Spirit to us is confirmed when we make a confession before the church that Jesus Christ is our Lord and Savior. With Paul we assume that no one can make this confession unless the Holy Spirit is at work in our lives (I Cor. 12:3).

So all members of our congregations do have the Holy Spirit from baptism and confirming confession onward. There is no question therefore of adding the Holy Spirit afterward as a so-called "second blessing." What does need to be added on the part of all members is the realization that it was the Spirit in their lives that made their confessions possible. But that is only the beginning. The best-kept secret in Christendom is that the Spirit who is already present in our lives strains to free the cornucopia of gospel blessings that the illusions of discipleship keep stopped up. Most church members live *as though* the Spirit were not present in their lives. They thus suppress most of her effects beyond confession except a dutiful pursuit of the precepts and example of Jesus.

Most of us are living as the disciples at Ephesus who missed receiving the Holy Spirit because they were baptized into John's baptism and had never even heard that

there was a Holy Spirit (Acts 19:1ff.). Given trinitarian
baptism, receipt of the Spirit is behind us. Transition to life
in the Spirit means coming to realize that the Spirit has
been present all along, pressing for fuller expression so
that the fruits of the Spirit may form on the otherwise
barren boughs of our trees of life. We are in the same
circumstances as Timothy. He had the gift within him by
nurture and by the laying on of hands but he needed to
rekindle the gift until it delivered him from timidity to
power, love, and self-control (II Tim. 1:4–7).

The church as body is the fellowship of those who together are coming to consciousness of being blessed by the
Spirit. Entrance into the church as body leaves the individual behind as the primary unit of God's graceful work.
In discipleship, individuals pursued their own advancement in competition with their companions—witness the
petitions of James and John and the question among the
Twelve about who was greatest. These isolated and competitive selves are left behind in the transition to Spirit,
and there emerge instead members of a body whose self
is Christ.

The graces for spiritual maturing are distributed
throughout the community in the form of complimentary
gifts. One can mature as an individual only by finding his
or her place within that community. Strictly speaking,
individuals do not mature; the community matures, and
individuals are drawn into the growth of the community.
Each member has an essential gift which it is the privilege
of each to discover and exercise within the community.
That is the first assignment that devotees of the Spirit have
in common. Now the full implication of the gift of the
Spirit unfolds. The Spirit is given not merely to assure the
individual Christian of fresh acceptance beyond humbling
and to lift up the believer into the incredible intimacy of
the circulation of divine life among Father, Son, and Spirit.
Beyond all that, each member is given a gift for equipping

the church as body with all the functions necessary to its maturing. The transition to Spirit completes itself as each member becomes aware of the Spirit in his or her life and identifies the particular function given to each for building up the church. Lists of such functions appear in three places within the Pauline school (I Cor. 12:7ff.; Rom. 12:6ff.; Eph. 4:11ff.) and once in I Peter 4:10ff. Mutual exercise of these functions makes maturing as a community the proximate goal of the Christian life. For this reason, although I am willing to grant that there may be salvation outside the church, there can be no maturing outside the church. Equipment for maturing is available only within that body.

Love's Body

It follows that the true charismatic is not a virtuoso performer drawing others after her or him like some spiritual Pied Piper, but a member of a community attuned to that community's needs. The New Testament does not have the word "charismatic." There are only the "charismata" or gifts that are "manifestations of the Spirit for the common good" (I Cor. 12:7). The lists of charismata all pertain to encouragement, consolation, and edification of the church (I Cor. 14).[57] In contrast to the Corinthian fascination with the unusual and miraculous, Paul ranked prophetic speaking highest among the charismata while including administration, acts of mercy, and the offering of funds.[58] This proves that the mark of the Spirit's presence in the church through member participation is not attested by supernatural in contrast to natural activity. That misconception in Corinth made ecstatic speaking in tongues seem the surest proof of the Spirit's presence. To correct this fascination with the miraculous and spectacular, Paul inserted the language of I Corinthians 13 into the discussion of spiritual gifts. The insertion declares that love is the only sure sign of the Spirit's presence. The Spirit engenders love in each member of the body to knit the body together. Gifts are mere instruments of love.

Paul's emphasis on love as the superlative mark of the Spirit's activity parallels John's refrain throughout the farewell discourses that the one new commandment Jesus leaves is that the disciples love one another (John 13: 34–35; 15:12, 17). The greatest miracle in the sphere of Spirit experience is the miracle of love (I Cor. 13:2). Since it is the presupposition and foundation of all manifestations of the Spirit, love's appearance is the surest sign of the Spirit's presence once there is confession of Jesus as Lord. It is the will of this Lord, above all, to love. As John insisted, that meant to love "one another"; to abide in Christ as the vine is to bear the fruit of loving the members of the Spirit community (John 15:7–12). Paul insisted on the same thing as he sought to deal with the pluralism of the Corinthian congregation, with Paul, Apollos, Cephas, or Christ as supposed champions of factions (I Cor. 1: 10–13). The apostle realized that unless the congregation could be united in love, the preaching of the gospel there would be frustrated by unloving competition. If, as we are maintaining, to become a Christian is to live a life and not merely to have a conversion experience, then the congregation must exemplify that life if it is to be the place where that life is nurtured.

Moltmann notes in connection with trinity that the image of God is a community of persons, Adam, Eve, and Seth, and not just the individual, Adam. Community is required for God to share blessings in the world. Community is the only adequate vehicle for God's presence. With the arrival in history of the Spirit community, the church as body replaced the nuclear family of Adam, Eve, and Seth. Now a congregation of devotees of Spirit, rather than the natural family, is the setting in which nurture for spiritual maturing takes place. Family membership does not entail the transition to life in the Spirit that is so necessary for such nurture.

The Johannine literature has been criticized for the emphasis it lays on love relationships within the believing community. This emphasis is often interpreted as a sign of sectarian separation from the world. John's community was committed to evangelize representatives of the whole broad spectrum of pluralism within Hellenistic culture. But unless the community could overcome the alienating factionalism of that pluralism with a Spirit-generated consensus, there could be no setting in which converts could mature. Without a love that rose above their differences, those in the church would remain only a baptized version of the pluralistic life of the world. Paul argued in effect for the same transcending of pluralism in his famous declaration: "There is neither Jew nor Greek, there is neither slave nor free, there is neither male nor female; for you are all one in Christ Jesus" (Gal. 3:28). Love bridges all of these distinctions.

So at both places in his epistles where Paul offered a list of charismata for the life of the church as body, love comes to the fore as the ground and aim of all giftedness (I Cor. 13; Rom. 12:9–10; 13:8–10). What makes this love so miraculous is that it is love for fellow and sister communicants whose weaknesses and failings are only too well known, not just love for strangers or new acquaintances whose shortcomings are still hidden. Apart from this love we try to get along with people in the congregation but settle eventually for wary tolerance and the protective distance of cliques. There a select, like-minded few qualify for the privilege of our caring acceptance and intimacy. This will not do. What the Spirit calls for, in Thomas Kelly's words, is for us to *"relove* our neighbors as ourselves." "The people we know best, see oftenest, have most to do with, these are *reloved* in a new and a deeper way."[59] In this reloving, the superlative miracle of life in the Spirit manifests itself within confessing communities. This makes possible the maturing which equips for mission.

Church Order Within the Body

Recognition of the church as the body of Christ composed of members mutually gifted by the Spirit for building up the community in love sets the stage for a radical reconception of church order. Until realization of the Spirit's presence dawns and mutual gifts are identified, the church is bound to order itself by rank.

Hierarchical order arises when ordained leaders operate as the only gifted persons in a crowd of disciples with little spiritual equipment. The crowd's main task is to gather passively to receive the benefit of the leader's charismata. This arrangement implies a qualitative distinction between clergy and laity. Our scheme of the Christian life reveals that this is really a distinction of phase of maturation. When disciples grow into giftedness, they can perform the functions of spiritual leadership as well.

Unless hierarchical ordering of churchly gatherings makes a place for another companion order more appropriate to a gifted *community,* the ordering necessitated by discipleship will inhibit maturing in the Spirit. In communities gathered as the body of Christ, Christ operating through the Spirit as head and source of life in the gathered body takes the place that clerical leadership must occupy in the discipleship phase. There is here a ranking of gifts according to the importance of their contribution to building up the body, but there is no longer any ranking of persons by office. From a human point of view the body is a leaderless group. Leadership circulates as the Spirit inspires those present in response to the issue at hand. "To each is given the manifestation of the Spirit for the common good" (I Cor. 12:7). When they come together then, "each one has a hymn, a lesson, a revelation, a tongue, or an interpretation," as all things are done for edification (I Cor. 14:26). This passage in I Corinthians and the similar one in Ephesians 5:18–20 offer glimpses of the church gathered under an ordering of the Spirit appropriate to the church as the body of Christ knit together and led by the Spirit.

Continuation of the Crucifixion

Transition to this kind of gathering after long practice of the rank and file ordering of discipleship will entail continuation of the crucifixion of self that launched entrance to life in the Spirit. Official leaders of disciples will have to suffer the crucifixion of the selves formed on the basis of clerical elevation within the local congregation and within the church at large. Disciples comfortable in the passive roles of listening observers and dependent followers will have to suffer the crucifixion of their passive selves as they accept responsibility for sharing leadership with the people. This reordering is bound to entail fear. Those defined as clergy will fear loss of status. Those defined as laity will fear inability to perform the new roles. The latter can take comfort in remembering that the Spirit has prayed through them when they did not know how to pray. They may expect the Spirit to lead through them when they have not known how to participate in leadership. Those with grace to risk body gatherings will find that as in everything else God works for good with those who love and who recognize the Spirit's mothering toward new levels of maturing.

No doubt a Spirit-generated order complicates the administration of a congregation where many, if not most, members are still in a discipleship phase of maturing. It means that two different church orders must be carried on simultaneously. We should not be put off. This is a familiar story in the history of the church. The Spirit has always

been forming an *ekklēsiola* within *ekklēsia*. What makes
them manageable is the recognition that both orders are
authentic expressions of church and that both are necessary to serve the whole spectrum of maturing. Each is
appropriate to the combination of levels of maturing of a
particular gathering. Care must be taken to encourage
and to enable disciples to gather in ways that supplement
the traditional Sunday morning service lest it become the
final form of churchly gathering. The same care must be
taken to encourage devotees of Spirit not to disdain gathering in common with everyone else on Sunday morning
so that the means of grace offered Sunday morning keep
check on the subjectivity of Spirit experiences. Sunday
morning worship is not just for the less mature. It is common worship for all phases of maturing. It is the place in
the life of a congregation where love binds the whole
congregation together. Members who disdain gathering
with the less mature reveal their own decline in spirituality.

Each congregation member deserves a continuing invitation to a place in a body group as well as to a particular
seat in the sanctuary for Sunday's common worship.
Maturing members will reserve places in both. The functions of smaller groups and common worship overlap.

The prospect of managing such a split-level church will
no doubt seem to many to be an impossible task. Administering and resourcing a one-level congregation is already
a 150 percent time commitment. To add another whole
set of meetings and programs may seem beyond human
limitations. The whole idea of keeping peace between the
mass of the congregation and the small groups who think
of themselves as maturing may make some pastors want to
reject this whole scheme out of hand. The leadership
called for here may seem beyond human capacity, but that
will be the key to its implementation. To begin with, there
is the call to "complete what is lacking in Christ's afflic-

tions for the sake of his body, that is, the church" (Col.
1:24). The greatest danger to pastors is not the complica-
tion these two orders bring to their lives. The greatest
danger is that by avoiding a Spirit order they will become
locked into the role of sole leader and forfeit the help for
ministry that the breeze of the Spirit brings.

From the point of view of disciple-leadership, stepping
aside to make way for the Spirit may seem like a come-
down as well as an invitation to chaos. From the point of
view of life in the Spirit it will mean rising to a level of
congregational life unattainable before. Nor should a
congregation expect less order when the Spirit leads.
"For God is not a God of confusion but of peace" (I Cor.
14:33).

Perhaps it only seems threatening beforehand. After
the fact, pastoral leaders may find themselves for the first
time in a position to receive ministry as well as give it. The
Spirit waits to comfort clergy as well as laity. After all,
placing oneself at the disposal of the Spirit through the
church as body is the answer to burnout. To offer one's
gifts in love for the maturing of the church as body *and to
receive the benefits of the loving gifts of others in return*
is what ministry is all about. To discern the body of Christ
in mutual ministry is as crucial as discerning the body in
the partaking of the Sacrament of the Lord's Supper. By
the same token, many of us are ill and weak, and some
have died, so far as maturing is concerned, precisely
through failure to discern the body in mutual ministry (I
Cor. 11:30).

Launching a Soma Group

Everyone knows what church looks like as it gathers for
Sunday morning worship. We have less experience with
groups that intend to take shape as the body of Christ. The

Greek word for body is *sōma,* so we call groups with this special intention "soma groups." What distinguishes them from other gatherings?

Soma group members have in common some experience of transition to life in the Spirit. That means they have come to see the difference between upward mobility and maturing in the Spirit. They are seeking to explore how that maturing works. They have come to realize that this maturing will require power beyond the self. They believe that this power is available in the Holy Spirit. They are seeking to make connection with the Spirit for this power in order to mature beyond the shaky beginnings of humiliation at the failure of discipleship. They live in fresh hope that a new level of life is in prospect. They have begun the startling identification of a chronic weakness in their makeup as Christians. They understand that they are gifted in some particular way so they can contribute to the group's maturing. They probably have not yet identified that particular gift. They may or may not have had practice in exercising it so that it benefits a group. Some probably have been exercising their gifts in the life of the congregation without identifying them as gifts of the Spirit. They understand that their maturing depends upon participation with others in something like a soma group. These distinguishing marks of soma members suggest an agenda.

Some groups might begin by recounting faith journeys that brought them to readiness for a soma gathering. The convener need not supply content for the group. The content is already there in the lives of the members. The convener's task is to facilitate a process by which members may comfortably share their faith stories with the group. The convener can also help the stories come out by asking questions that refer to the facets of experience I have mentioned above that make up transition to life in the

Spirit and maturing in the church. As the members hear from one another the Spirit finds opportunity to confirm, encourage, and draw each member and the group as a whole on to greater maturing. The group obviously must be small.

I would not expect a soma group to form in a parish until the pastoral leader has done considerable preaching, teaching, and counseling about life in the Spirit and about the marks of the church as the body of Christ. The pastor must also have followed up public discussion with pastoral conversations that have elicited faith stories. Probably the first soma group in a parish should form by personal invitation from the pastor after he or she has heard enough faith stories of prospective members to be reasonably sure they are ready with the elements of experience and consciousness that characterize a soma group.

The group should begin as a contract group. Members contract to share their faith journeys in weekly meetings for as long as it takes for each person's faith story to be told with leisure. *In these first weeks of the group's life I would not allow members to offer help to one another unless someone asks for specific help.* I would make that a ground rule. The first stage of the group's life is for listening. To begin with, that will be help enough.

After all the stories of the group are out, then I would ask the members what they found helpful in hearing the stories of others, and, only after that, what each found difficult to understand or accept. "I" statements would be the norm, rather than "you" statements with their implied judgment. The initial contract period would close with an opportunity for each member to say whether he or she wishes to continue into the next contract period. The contract in the next stage would be to begin to explore how to help one another in a common quest for maturing in the Spirit.

In addition to assembling the group by invitation, the pastor would probably want to tell her or his story early on to model the procedure of sharing. After that the main business of the convener would be to monitor the process to see that it kept to the group's contract.

The group should open with a brief devotional period on some aspect of life in the Spirit. Time should be set aside in each session when the group would meditate together in silence. Begin and close with a hymn or song. I would close the silent prayer portion with the Lord's Prayer in common. Spontaneous group participation in prayer would fit the second stage when members had contracted for greater intimacy.

This is enough to indicate the initial stage of the life of a soma group. Its beginning focus would be the life stories of the members. All together these would amount to the story of the activity of the Spirit in the lives of the group so far. It would also amount to the beginning of the story of the life of the Spirit in the group as a group in process of becoming the body of Christ.

The second contract stage would concentrate on discovering the disciplines that facilitate life lived consciously under the empowering, comforting guidance of the Holy Spirit. The group would agree to reinforce the discipline of Bible study, devotional reading, and prayer and meditation that each member is developing. In that context the group would offer help in overcoming obstacles to practicing the presence of God in the Spirit. At this point the group would begin to exercise the gifts they had begun to identify in the initial stage. In addition to continuing the format of the first stage, each weekly session would end with a go-around for each person to say what help the session had been that time. These suggestions address nurture, only one of the two foci of a soma group. The other focus of a soma group is mission.

PART II: MATURING IN MISSION

Worldwide and Cosmic Scope of Mission

Whether gathered with a body group on a Sunday morning in a sanctuary or on a weekday evening, the sojourner in maturing only pauses there. Church gatherings are not the final destination of the journey of faith. The journey of faith is ultimately a journey in mission. The church is a training facility or staging area to launch members into mission, a M*A*S*H unit to return them to service when they are wounded in the line of duty, a rest area in which they can catch the breath of the Spirit when fatigue in mission sets in. "There remains a sabbath rest for the people of God," says the writer of Hebrews, but that final rest is not here, not now (Heb. 4:9).

Paul probably invented the idea of the church as the "body of Christ."[60] He makes clear that its ultimate function is not upbuilding for its own sake. The church as Christ's body is the vehicle of Christ's mission to the world.

The church in mission lies at the root of Paul's whole understanding of his apostleship. The great contribution of Eduard Schweizer's fresh appreciation of Romans is to enable us to see that the book did not arise primarily to teach the doctrine of justification by faith to disciples struggling under the burden of producing their own righteousness, but as an expression of Paul's implementation of the church's calling to be the missionary body of Christ.[61] The thrust of the letter and the church consciousness it represents is summed up in Rom. 1:16: "For I am not ashamed of the gospel: it is the power of God for salvation to every one who has faith, to the Jew first and also to the Greek." Although Paul was not personally acquainted with the church of Rome, he fully expected that as church the people would sympathize and support him in the common mission to spread the gospel where it had never been heard by Gentiles (Rom. 15:15–21). In this case it meant support to go to Spain (Rom. 15:24).

In Colossians and Ephesians the mission of the church as "body" takes on cosmic dimensions. The author revises the hymn at the base of Colossians 1:15–20 so as to make Christ the creator and reconciler of all creation. As a by-product of this cosmic reconciliation the gospel has in principle already been declared from heaven to every creature (Col. 1:23; Eph. 3:9–10). The task of the church as "body" is to implement this cosmic principle with the concrete preaching of the gospel to the whole world and especially to the Gentiles (Col. 1:27; Eph. 2:11–19).

Christians are destined to be missionaries. We were warned from the beginning. Before the first four who were called to discipleship knew quite what they were getting into, Jesus had declared that they would continue to be fishermen, only it would be people they would catch (Mark 1:17; Matt. 4:19; Luke 5:10). Jesus modeled this missionary, fishing function from the beginning.

For the sake of presentation I have concentrated the consideration of mission toward the end of this discussion. That was not the order in which mission was experienced in the New Testament church. Wherever and whenever men and women began the journey of faith it was always in the context of the mission already in progress. Jesus recruited and trained disciples while he was engaged in the mission. New Testament Christians were always missioners in on-the-job training.

While the disciples were granted some time to observe and listen, they were soon put into mission themselves as extensions of the ministry of Jesus. This occurred long before they had experienced the maturing enlightenment of the transition to life in the Spirit. Even at an immature stage they were able to do exorcism and healing, although their preaching of the kingdom of God must have been distorted by their misunderstanding of it. The lesson is that it is better to risk the errors immature disciples will make while engaging in mission than delay participation until disciples are more mature. What is to be avoided is the impression that mission is optional. Jesus gave the first disciples authority to engage in mission despite their immaturity (Matt. 10:1; Mark 6:7; Luke 9:1). *Mission engagement is an obligation in every phase of the journey of faith.*

Worldwide mission is mandated or assumed by every New Testament author. In Mark, world mission fills the time until the return of the Son of man (Mark 13:10). The result of that mission will be that when the Son of man comes there will be elect to be gathered "from the four winds, from the ends of the earth to the ends of heaven" (Mark 13:27). Matthew's great commission fills the same time with the worldwide ministry-in-mission of the disciples until "the close of the age" (Matt. 28:18–20). Luke also filled the time until the end with the church in mission "to the end of the earth" (Acts 1:8). John's departing Christ sent the disciples into the world for mission just as he had been sent (John 17:18). Their whole function under the Paraclete was to be witnesses (15:27). Worldwide and transcultural mission in John's community is implied by the arrival of Greek inquirers (12:20–22) and by the trilingual declaration over a crucifixion (19:20) designed "to draw everyone" to him (12:32). The authors cited represent a consensus of the New Testament church. To be a Christian is to be engaged in one way or another in world mission.

The mission went forward primarily by the preaching of a cadre of apostles and prophets appointed to this special function. Still their ministry depended on the recognition,

commission, financial support, and hospitality of the rank
and file of local congregations. The prophetic witness to
the gospel depended for its authentication upon the quality of life of these local communities. Even when a disciplelike understanding of church order put charismatic
figures alone in leadership roles, the witness of every individual was still crucial. Members were recruited continually for this confirming witness. That is the force of the
commission to the cured demoniac from the country of
the Gerasenes: "Go home to your friends, and tell them
how much the Lord has done for you, and how he has had
mercy on you" (Mark 5:19). In obeying that commission
the cured demoniac fulfilled the equivalent of a prophet's
ministry. Mark called his confirming witness "proclamation" (Mark 5:20).

At the more advanced stage of maturing in mission the
distinction between prophetic and ordinary witness
disappears. We have seen how this happens when the
church becomes a body of mutually gifted believers.
Paul's letters show he had fellow workers—traveling
companions, such as Epaphroditus (Phil. 2:25; 4:18), and
people in every local congregation, such as Aquila and
Prisca (I Cor. 16:19; Rom. 16:3–5)—who seem to have
shared the mission fully with him though they were not
bearers of any office. They were people who had heeded
Paul's advice to seek the gift of prophecy above all others, and their prayers had been answered (I Cor. 14:1).
The lesson in all this is clear. In every phase of the Christian life, those who are willing to participate in the mission of the church to the extent of their ability grow and
mature. By the same token, apart from mission, spiritual
growth stops and atrophy sets in. This lesson is a familiar
one. What is not so well understood is how we get from
New Testament mandates for mission to the modern
mandate for social change.

Social Mission

The cured demoniac reminds us that healing accompanied the proclamation as a standard feature of mission. These healings, as the constant accompaniment of oral witness, symbolize the fact that the church in mission always took care of every human need at the same time that it offered the particular blessing of salvation. This "second mile," beyond the formal obligation of religious propaganda common to every other religion of New Testament times, was what made the mission effective. I am sure John Gager is largely correct when he accounts for the success of Christianity in the competition with its rivals by the fact that it was social as well as religious.[62] That implied, among other things, total care for the neighbors to whom the mission was brought. A Roman emperor put his finger on this caring as the factor that made the church's witness so effective. "Why do we not observe that it is their benevolence to strangers, their care for the graves of the dead, and the pretended holiness of their lives that has done the most to increase atheism [he meant Christianity]? It is disgraceful that when no Jew ever has to beg, and the impious Galileans support not only their own but ours as well, all men see that our people lack aid from us."[63] This care for the needy (Matt. 25:34–39), coupled with the oral witness, made the mission effective. This is the point that growth evangelism tends to overlook.

Care in the early missionary church was not so obsessively interpersonal that it lost track of the sociocreational context that determined the quality of personal life. As Christiaan Beker takes pains to point out, Paul looked forward to the redemption of all creation to which our bodies now bind us in premillennial groaning (Rom. 8: 22–23).[64] Not only Pauline thought but the whole apocalyptic undercurrent of the New Testament assumes that salvation for individuals is inconceivable without a transformation of the structures of society and creation; therefore the indispensable hope of the end. The promise in Colossians and Ephesians of the redemption of life from the tyranny of the principalities and powers carries out this same concern for the sociostructural side of life in terms of Hellenistic cosmology (Eph. 3:10; 6:12; Col. 1:16; 2:15).

This cosmic, sociocreational dimension of redemption grounds the modern mandate for social change. The lordship of Christ in the present is already working toward the transformation of social structure. Christ will complete this project only at the end, but he is engaged in it already. His body, the church, must engage in it with him. The principalities and powers that oppose God come to expression in the social forces that social structures embody. All Christians are obligated by connection with Christ to work for social structures that embody his blessed reign.

The Risks of Social Mission

Taking missionary responsibility for the sociostructural context of life is what makes participation in mission so risky. When those who depend upon existing structures for "the good life" detect that the church's mission involves shaking up these very structures, a profound change of attitude sets in. Engaging in mission becomes dangerous. The resistance of those who benefit from existing structures is what tradition calls persecution. When the Roman emperor Julian described Christians as "atheist" and "impious," he meant they were subversives who threatened the social and political structures of the Roman Empire.

In the light of these structural implications of mission, the cross becomes as relevant to service in mission to the world as it was to maturation within the church—only now it has much more direct correlation with Jesus' crucifixion. As we grow in faith the significance of the cross for the journey of faith shifts. To begin with, it appeared at the Lord's Supper to provide in some unspecified way forgiveness "for many." Then in Gethsemane it blocked the way to religious upward mobility and came to symbolize the death of the self formed by that enterprise. In the church as the body of Christ the cross came to mean the extending of self-denial to incorporation into a community where the personal religious quest of each member was subordinated to the upbuilding in love of the whole. Finally, in risky mission the meaning of the cross comes full circle as the world's response to those who, like their Lord, not only reject the world's way of life but also bring the critical and transforming witness of the gospel to bear on the structures that support and define that worldly way. In short, when loving witness escalates to a concern for justice, as it must in the maturing missioner, the church as missionary body of Christ will seem as threatening to the world as Jesus did in his original mission in his original body.

From the world's point of view it was bad enough when the early church only witnessed to the imminent but future transformation of the structures of the world by a final act of God at the end. When the church takes steps to implement some degree of that transformation *now,* the reaction escalates. To accept with love the suffering that this reaction entails, still rejoicing in the grace of God, is a sure sign of maturing.

The full scope of loving mission to the world is threefold: verbal proclamation of and testimony to the gospel (witness); relief of every human need we encounter (charity); challenge, reformation, and re-creation of all of the social structures of life that affect the well-being of each member of society (social action). The New Testament is full of the first two. The expectation of the end eclipsed the third although it is witnessed to in the renewal of creation and society promised as part of that end. With the passing of time and the realization that the structures of society are of our own making, concern to implement justice now must take its place as equal in importance to witness and charity. If love has its way with us, we must realize, sooner or later, that passing out cups of cold water to thirsty neighbors is no substitute for a public water system; that coming to the imprisoned is no loving substitute for legal aid if the imprisoned ought not to be there in the first place; that visitation of the sick is no substitute for a system of adequate medical care available to all.

To mature in mission is to be willing to engage in witness, charity, and action for justice simultaneously whatever the risk in loss of worldly status and reward. Maturing in mission means becoming willing to grow to the place where we are relatively indifferent to the punishing reaction our efforts may inspire in some. Even Jesus' opponents begrudgingly admired this indifference. "Teacher, we know that you are true and care for no man; for you do not regard the position of men, but truly teach the way of God" (Mark 12:14).

It takes some time to mature to this point. When Paul first encountered opposition from the representative of the dominant social structure in Arabia, his gospel apparently had challenged the final authority of King Aretas. When persecution set in, the novice missionary became a basket case, turning tail to run for safety to Jerusalem. In retrospect he recognized that as a genuine weakness (II Cor. 11:30ff.). He grew beyond that weakness, as subsequent imprisonments prove. It is indicative of Paul's final maturing that the church last remembered him as in prison making the most of his opportunity to preach the gospel and generalizing from his lifelong maturing in mission: "All who desire to live a godly life in Christ Jesus will be persecuted" (II Tim. 3:12). The world notes when the missioner is willing to pay a price to witness. This willingness to risk loss seals the sincerity of the witness in the eyes of a world suspicious of every kind of huckster.

The greatest obstacle to maturing in the American churches in our time comes from our division into parties, one of which practices witness and charity to the exclusion of acts of justice, while the other practices justice and charity to the exclusion of witness. Maturing in church and in mission means creating "one new person in place of [these] two, so making peace" as surely as reconciliation in the first century meant a new person created out of the party heritage of Jew and Gentile (Eph. 2:15).

Intimacy with God in Christ by the Spirit binds all three facets of mission together. Out of Spirit intimacy the willing missioner is led to see which facet of mission is appropriate to each occasion. The party of the church committed to witness and charity is familiar with this guidance, but their prejudice usually has excluded guidance to action for justice. On the other hand, those committed to action for justice usually scorn the piety of intimacy and the guidance associated with it. We need to recover the wholeness of maturing in mission modeled in the life of one of the authentic saints of the American church, the Quaker, John Woolman. It was precisely intimacy with God and the guidance flowing from it that led him to the "concern" for freeing slaves in colonial America. That piety guided him to simplify his business and family life so that they would serve the "concern" that grew upon him until he became a one-man abolition society traversing the colonies to act for justice in the case of slaves.[65]

Maturing piety eventually leads each of us to a "concern" for some aspect of justice in the world that becomes a lifelong missionary calling giving special point and focus to love for the world. Only God can bear the care of all the fronts for justice in the world. In mercy God distributes that care in modest, individual-sized bundles to match the gifts for mission the Spirit bestows on each of us. No one ought to suppose that he or she has received the full experience of the journey of faith until having received his or her bundle. But the bundle comes with no promise of resounding success.

Patience

Faith, hope, and love abide. We have seen how faith leads to intimacy and intimacy to an appreciation of the greatest of these, love. We have seen how love grounds all that the maturing believer does in church and in mission. But, finally, the maturing sojourner lives in hope, for none of the great projects of justice worth attempting in faith and love ever comes to completion in this world. We have been adequately warned of this by Paul's description of the Spirit as "first fruits" and "down payment" (Rom. 8:23; II Cor. 1:22; 5:5). This does not imply that the Spirit has been given to us only in part, that God withholds something of the Spirit from us here and now. It means that the Spirit is a power from the age to come when the purposes of God will be completely realized in a way that is impossible under the circumstances of this age. What one hopes for in this life is the grace to stay in the service of one's "concern" in spite of all discouragement at the lack of results. The hope that social transformation will happen in God's good time, though we may not live to see it, enables us to wait for it with patience (Rom. 8:25). This connection of patience and hope makes the triad of faith, love, and steadfastness (Titus 2:2) just as apt as the one in I Corinthians 13.[66] Those are the virtues recommended especially for "the elder," which means the more mature, person. A decisive mark of maturing is the strength to stay lifelong with an unfinished mission assignment. This is no human achievement but is a gift from God. Its mood is joy and thanksgiving rather than Stoic apathy (Col. 1:11–12). John Woolman knew the gift of "looking less at the Effects of my Labor, than at the Motion

and Reality of the concern as it arises from heavenly Love"
with the result that when he continued to follow his God-
given concern "in Patience and Meekness, heavenly Peace
is the Reward of our Labors."

Completing the Soma Group's Agenda

The soma group resembles a parabola with two foci. As
we saw above, the initial focus is nurture. The culminating
focus is mission. The risen Christ is as restless to get on
with the mission in his second incarnation in the church
as he was in his first incarnation as the historical Jesus. "Let
us go on to the next towns, that I may preach there also;
for that is why I came out" (Mark 1:38). "I cast out demons
and perform cures today and tomorrow, and the third day
I finish my course. Nevertheless I must go on my way
today and tomorrow and the day following" (Luke 13:
32–33). Luke dramatized the shift from one focus to another in his portrayal of the soma group in the upper room
in Jerusalem. At first they concentrated on the nurture
focus in prayer (Acts 1:12–14). Then the mission focus ex-
ploded on them in the form of Pentecost (Acts 2:1ff.). The
parabola pattern completed itself.

This stage of the life of a soma group features a contract
to share the ways in which the sites where members live,
work, and do their politics offer opportunity for mission.
At last we come to the goal of all institutional church life
—the ministry of the laity in the world. Everything that
happens within the institution up until this point is mere
preparation. The agenda of the group now becomes the
relating of the circumstances of each member's life as
these circumstances call for witness, charity, and justice.
What is called for? What is each attempting? What is working? What is not? How shall we be strengthened to attempt what we are afraid to try? How shall we proceed to
meet the opportunities that we clearly see?

Now the group must tap the gifts and graces of all to meet the challenges that mission brings. The time for merely listening is over. Help must be offered. If the problems that emerge are beyond the resources of the group, then they must decide together where to go to get the help they need.

The prayer and meditation that is already a feature of the group's life will now take up the problems and challenges of each person's mission. Some mission opportunities call for study and research. There will be homework to do. The group will become a study group as well as a discussion group, a prayer group, and a workshop for mission. In the measure to which the group embraces the work of both nurture and mission foci, it is coming to share the work of the pastoral leader. *In soma groups the laity come to share the ministry of the church professional.*

The End of Clerical Isolation

As the institution structures it, the task of the church leader is the loneliest profession in the world. Although in theory the ministry of the church belongs to the whole people of God, until soma groups emerge the minister does the church's ministry almost single-handedly. The laity just receive that ministry. With time this arrangement becomes an intolerable burden, for no one member of the body has the gifts and graces necessary to carry out the whole ministry of nurture and mission for the church. God has distributed the gifts and graces for the church's ministry throughout its ranks, clergy and laity included. But until a soma group forms, the gifts and graces of the laity remain mostly untapped. Laity choke in their development at a point where they scarcely suspect they have any gifts and graces to offer. With the emergence of soma members as gifted missioners, the clergyperson finally gets the comradeship in ministry that good theologies of ministry promise but that the institutional church is simply not structured to deliver. If they emerge soon enough, soma groups are the clergyperson's best insurance against burnout and mid-career crisis. If these emerge later, the soma groups are the best remedy.

Churches for the Unchurched Clergy

Clergypersons need soma groups to fulfill their ministry as much as laypersons do. The institutional church structures the role of the parish leader so that he or she is practically unchurched. The pastor is forever dispensing the means of grace but only rarely receives them. Most clergy cannot worship well while leading worship. Even fewer clergy can hear the Word of God adequately through their own preaching. This is why clergy are so starved for common worship when they gather for continuing education events. They have been accumulating hunger for the means of grace for months!

The only answer to nurture for clergy so that they are enabled to fulfill their ministries is for them to take the initiative to form soma groups of their own. Unless clergy do this for themselves they are bound to deteriorate in their own spiritual maturation as well as in their capacity to minister. The bitter irony is that Protestant clergy are the least churched members of their churches although they are always in church. The constant offering of the means of grace largely passes them by. It is as though the world's famous chefs, as a group, suffered from malnutrition bordering on starvation. Clergy must come out of the kitchen and sit at table to be fed like the rest. Their table will be the soma group composed of clergy who follow the same staged agenda we have suggested for everyone else in the church. At this table the personal trauma and crisis that the institution builds into the profession as now constituted can be eased or prevented by

the same good news and divine care we see our parishioners enjoy.

For clergy, the first stage of the agenda will include
relating the call to ministry and the meaning of that call
to each as part of personal stories of faith. Nurture for
clergy will include tips and encouragement from one another for mastery of the various roles the institution ex-
pects of its professional leaders. Getting good at what they
are required to do is the foundation of respect and self-
esteem that permits further development.

Performing the roles that the institution calls for, however, does not yet shift the clergyperson to the mission
focus. That happens when pastors start to turn parish ministry outward to the world where unchurched people are.
Only when clergy too engage the world in witness, charity, and justice, thereby escaping the ghetto of the institutional church, does their soma group become the body of
Christ with its peculiar gifts and graces. In this they are
just like laity.

The ultimate agenda item for clergy gathered as body
of Christ will be finding how to lead the parishioners as
individuals and as a congregation to fulfill their mission in
the world. The resistance that arises within the congregation to this definition of its reason for being will be the
modern clergyperson's equivalent of the persecution that
arose within Judaism to the ministries of Jesus and the
early church. I do not expect, however, that we need to
anticipate martyrdom as the final seal of our ministries. If
we offer our parishioners the chance to grow spiritually,
they will come to see this meaning for themselves, just as
clergy have. Thus everything depends on our skill and
commitment in turning the roles assigned to clergy within
the institution into occasions to nurture parishioners toward maturing in the church as body of Christ in mission
beyond the institution. In terms of master role, the prophetic guide makes strategic use of each professional role

to offer the resources for laity to mature in the Christian life. Maturing parishioners will come to see that the institution is worth the trouble it takes to support and maintain only when it serves their ministry in the world. Let us see what this means role by role for the pastoral leader as prophetic guide.

CHAPTER 5
ORGANIZING FOR MATURING

The Payoff of the Master Role

The master role pays off in the measure to which it organizes all subordinate roles into a satisfying strategic unity. The role of prophetic guide has that capacity. It promises satisfaction of the minister's primary calling to be a prophet-pastor rather than an institutional functionary. It promises satisfaction for clergy who aim to share the church's ministry with the whole people of God to whom that ministry properly belongs. It promises to move the ministry of the congregation out beyond the boundaries of the institution to the world Christ longs to contact through his body, the church. It promises a way for clergy to recover control of a profession that increasingly leaves them at the mercy of demands on their time and energy that have marginal relationship to the heart of their calling. Consistently applied, the master role offers a way to fend off the mid-career crisis to which the vast majority of us seem programmed in almost fateful manner. Practiced consistently and with integrity, the master role of prophetic guide gives a chance to assert control over the crazy quilt of incessant demands placed on the pastoral leader in a typical twelve- to thirteen-hour day. I am convinced that it is this merciless and fraying chaos of demands that produces burnout. A master role in which our calling finds deeply felt expression would allow us to rest confidently when we are led to say no and to get the full, joyful energy of our calling behind the things to which we say yes. Above all, we would now take the initiative to organize our work to fulfill our calling rather than being organized by demands into which we fit our calling somehow willy-nilly.

What follows should be taken as suggestive—a very broad hint. Each pastoral leader will know best what fits his or her situation and unique sense of calling. If you find yourself reacting, "Oh, no—that won't work! Here would be the way to accomplish that," I will be delighted. Finally, each of us will have to define his or her own calling. There is no cookie-cutter solution to such a personal matter. Let us hope that in the end we shall all become gracefully eccentric.

The Guide as Preacher-Liturgist

The master role of prophetic guide shapes the major roles required of the pastoral leader so that in each of them the goal sought is that of maturing in the Christian life. The most prominent role is, of course, preacher-liturgist. It is a good place to begin. Whether or not this role is of primary importance to clergy in their personal theologies of ministry, it is the one the congregation experiences most often. Therefore it signals most loudly what the leader intends the main business of a congregation to be.

Preaching from the lectionary or some adaptation of it can make the church year display the whole span of maturing in the Christian life and offer appropriate invitations to maturing along the way. Beginning with Advent, the situation that called Christmas into being in the first place, sets the Christian life theme.

Christmas was invented to counter the pagan festival of

the birth of the sun-god. The danger was that Christians were being drawn into the orbit of the gods of fate represented by the implacable round of the solar year. Christ's birth was celebrated to present him as a figure superior in every way to the central figures of this competing religion. In terms of the sweep of the Christian life, Christmas becomes the great evangelistic festival of the church year. Surely, the act of the Godhead in bringing to birth the destined savior and ruler of the world in such humble fashion is the single most winsome moment in redemptive history. The aim of the sermons and liturgies of Advent and Christmastide would be to show Christ as the fulfillment of Israel's and all humankind's hopes for personal salvation and social redemption, for peace of heart and peace on earth. Epiphany then becomes the culminating illustration of the drawing power of this incomparable figure when all the nations of the earth offer their allegiance in the gifts of the Wise Men.

Jesus' baptism and the call of the first disciples follow Epiphany in the lectionary. This dual event becomes an invitation to baptism and church membership. Communicants classes would graduate into church membership as their committed response to the call to discipleship or perhaps as part of an Epiphany pageant. Epiphany season would be the period to lay down the fundamental character, obligations, and privileges of discipleship as they are summarized, for example, in the Sermon on the Mount.

Lent would expand on the explanation of discipleship through the unfolding ministry of Jesus for new church members and for the less mature already in the congregation. At the same time Lent would emphasize the challenge to confessing Christians of long standing for deeper repentance and faith called for by the events in Passion Week. The tragedy and triumph of Good Friday and Easter would become the occasion to invite everyone to some particular facet of transition to life in the Spirit.

At this point the preacher-liturgist would be careful to make clear that the phases of the Christian life are not something each person negotiates only once. Rather, it is a series that we repeat each time a new appreciation of the demand and promise of the gospel throws fresh light on areas of our lives that our journey toward maturing has not yet touched or not touched deeply enough. Prayer as practice of the presence of God; reloving of family, workmates, and church members; compassion for the oppressed and disadvantaged; unmasking of the world's claims of God's sanction for its unjust structures; integrity of mission interweaving witness, acts of mercy, and acts of justice: all are areas of continuing growth in grace as long as we live. Lent would be the time when we are led to further work of maturing in such areas.

My suggestion replaces the traditional practices of graduating communicants classes at Easter. When Lent first developed, churches were in a setting of persecution where church membership in and of itself inevitably required a break with the world. In our time a conscious break with the world comes later in the Christian life, if at all. We need a festival that marks that crucial step toward maturing. Lent seems uniquely fitted to dramatize that move.

Pentecost would be the time for new repentance and new purpose, coupled with fresh appropriation of the power of the Spirit. The promise of baptism with the Holy Spirit hangs over discipleship. Pentecost is a natural invitation to appropriate that promise with concrete realizations of the presence of the Spirit in the lives of disciples who had been pursuing their faith journey pretty much by their own power. It would also be the most appropriate festival for the celebration of the birth of the church as the body of Christ. The Christian life then becomes the journey of a community swept along by the breeze of the Spirit rather than the solo efforts of struggling individuals.

Perhaps the Lord's Supper should receive its strongest emphasis at this season rather than at Easter when, by tradition, new members take their first Communion. In a Pentecost setting the Lord's Supper dramatizes incorporation into church as the body of Christ.

Pentecost would be the time to introduce and reinforce the idea that the church must gather in small clusters in order to mature. It would be the time to open up old groups to new participants. Existing groups could renegotiate their contracts with new configurations of leadership, fresh curricula, and expanded mission—emphasizing that the call to mission extends to every area and location of life. Preaching and liturgy would constantly recall that the church executes mission. Individuals act as commissioned extensions of this missionary task force. The unifying theme of the long Pentecost season would be church in mission in the power of the Spirit.

The Pentecost season spans the vacation months of summer. Usually this means taking a vacation from churchly concerns. Rather than seeing summer as a time to withdraw, members could use these months to devote some of their vacation time to sharing in missionary work projects, or at least visiting church mission projects near their vacation sites. In the fall they would report back to the congregation. Summer could become a fruitful time for mission emphasis. Mission work and study tours might even come to compete with conventional vacation junkets.

Pentecost begins to reveal the liturgist's task as twofold. We need Sunday morning liturgies when worshipers are in an audience mode typical of discipleship, and we need soma group liturgies for smaller gatherings where worshipers are in a participatory mode typical of the transition to life in the Spirit and of maturing in the church and in mission. Resources are rich for traditional Sunday morning worship. What needs to be developed are worship formats that encourage each member of an assembled body to identify his or her special gifts and to offer them for mutual encouragement and edification. I Corinthians 14:26–33 and Ephesians 5:18–20 offer a window on such gatherings. In these gatherings spontaneous leadership by the Spirit prompts participation for the common good. Here formats for worship encourage and order spontaneous leading. In the Pauline churches official leaders such as apostles, prophets, and teachers were present, but in the act of gathered worship their role as leaders was muted by the Spirit's urging and prompting of contributions by every group member. Comparable liturgies of Spirit-led groups need to be invented to provide vehicles of maturing in our day; otherwise, conventional Sunday morning worship will tend to freeze worshipers into nonparticipation and thereby arrest members at less mature stages of faith.

The soma form of liturgy can never displace the traditional Sunday morning hour. Participating in a soma group liturgy requires a consciousness of Spirit and community and an accompanying discipline which are beyond the reach of most church members. For their sake and for the sake of inquirers after faith, the preaching service will continue to be central. But even in these liturgies elements can be included that invite movement toward greater participation and maturing. Laypeople reading Scripture lessons, serving in choirs, providing instrumental music, and performing various liturgical tasks announce that the life of this congregation and its leadership are shared by clergy and laity. "Minutes for mission" or a comparable form of regular reporting by laypeople of mission and maturing projects carried out by laypeople, including reports from soma groups, can set the Sunday morning worship in the context of the whole church's life so that worshipers see Sunday morning as an introduction to the life of faith rather than its main event.

The eventual goal would be for each church member to find it normal to attend both Sunday morning preaching services and a participatory soma group at some other time of the week. Meanwhile the main aim of the preacher-liturgist would be to keep the *whole* spectrum of the Christian life and of the church's mission before the crowd that gathers on Sunday morning regardless of how the individuals may be spread across the spectrum of maturing.

A rounded and well-designed liturgy is itself a major vehicle for displaying the whole range of the phases of maturing. A careful setting of the presence of God as context for divine service models what the aim of transition in Spirit is. Prayers of adoration, praise, and thanksgiving for the Godhead in and of themselves may pass over the heads of most congregants. However, such prayers keep announcing the ultimate aim of Christian life before everyone as an invitation to maturing. Likewise a trinitarian liturgy offers the full blessing of the nurture of the Godhead although some may be ready only for the masculine or feminine role equivalents of God's parenting and partnering. Just as the reports of ongoing mission keep the full range of the mission before the whole congregation, so a liturgy with theological and experiential integrity keeps the full range of maturing in God constantly before the whole congregation. Worshipers never outgrow such a liturgy—they just keep growing into it.

If the dominant aim of the preacher-liturgist is to keep the whole gospel before every gathering of the congregation, sooner or later the congregation must take into account what makes that gospel interesting and relevant. The question of the relevance of the gospel finds its answer in the two major ministerial roles of pastor and guide to mission in community.

The Guide as Pastor

Perhaps in no other area of clerical practice do the master role of prophetic guide to maturing in the Christian life

and the professional role called for by the institution blend
so nearly into one as in the case of the minister as pastor.
The institution designates the congregational leader as
spiritual guide for each member of the congregation.
Among Protestants this is an unfamiliar role for which
most clergy have no training or model. This is being
remedied as seminaries begin to accept responsibility in
this area,[67] but clergy now in place must scramble for
resourcing.

What complicates the acquiring of skill in this role is the
resourcing already in place for the pastor as psychological
counselor rather than as spiritual guide. Many clergy
themselves have experienced psychological counseling or
have been trained for it. The role model of clergyperson
as psychological counselor is very familiar. This creates
difficulty when the pastor as guide to psychological maturing eclipses the pastor as guide to Christian maturing. The
eclipse of the pastor as spiritual guide is partly a result of
the fact that the therapeutic community has a much
clearer notion of psychological maturing and how to move
to it than the theological community has of Christian
maturing and the way to move in that direction. This book
is an attempt to help remedy that vagueness about Christian maturing.[68]

Perhaps a good enough definition of psychological
maturing is the increasing capacity to love deeply and
work productively. The means for this is a deepening ac-
quaintance with the patterns of feeling and acting that
one has acquired in relation to the important persons in
one's own psychic history, coupled with a deepening appreciation of the worth of one's self. A therapist acts as a
guide in the use of these means. A companion definition
of Christian maturing would be an increasing capacity to
love God and neighbor and to work in a calling to spread
the reign of God. The means for this are membership in
a church community and full use of the means of grace.

The pastoral leader acts as guide in the use of these means.

The point I wish to highlight by this comparison is that these maturings are not the same thing. What fairly leaps to attention is that while a vast array of professionals in our society, including clergy, are participating in one way or another to serve psychological maturing, our society assigns no one to attend to spiritual maturing. That is the sole prerogative of clergy. Herein lies our distinctive identity and unique worth. No other profession or combination of professions can replace us in this function. We clergy ought to bask in the warmth of that knowledge until we glow with appropriate pride in our distinctive calling. Too many clergy try to live off composite identities borrowed from functions we have in common with other helping professions. This can only yield low self-esteem. We are not certified and recognized members of these other professions. We are mostly amateurs and dilettantes in the functions that we share with so many of them. Strong self-esteem and high morale lie in celebrating our distinctive calling and in vigorously pursuing the special expertise that belongs to it.

I am convinced that the first major step to expertise as a guide to maturing in the Christian life is to listen to as many stories of faith journeys among members of one's congregation as pastoral access provides. Next, the stories must be analyzed according to a theory of Christian maturing. Then the pastor needs to imagine ways and means to further maturing.

We are talking here about more data than can be safely entrusted for accuracy to any pastor's memory. I can see no other alternative than the one used in the other helping professions, namely, the keeping of records of personal histories as they are taken. This raises the issues of confidentiality, access to records, etc. Other professions have evolved practices that resolve those issues. I am confident we can as well. We must be about the business of learning and recording just how the Christian life is being lived by the people for whom we are responsible. No amount of casual observation and general cultural analysis can substitute for hearing particular stories.

The taking of case histories in the form of listening to stories of faith journeys not only increases the capacity of the pastor to understand and serve the parishioner but also tends to stimulate maturing in the faithful by raising to consciousness the crucial factors in maturing. Imagine the focus it would give the life of a congregation to have the pastoral leader making appointments to hear life journeys. We might begin with leadership first. Applicants for membership and members of communicants classes would be next. Interviews of faith journeys could follow up consultation for acute problems. These interviews should become a part of the procedure of pastoral calling in homes and hospitals. Telling and hearing faith journeys would have the effect of declaring a partnership in maturing on the part of pastor and parishioner. An interviewing schedule can be extrapolated from the sketch of maturing in the last three chapters. A sample schedule in Appendix II represents a beginning in this direction.

A review of the case histories in hand would enhance the pastoral care of these people in times of crisis. The aim would be to develop the full resources of the phases of maturing already active for support in the crisis. At the same time the pastor guide would be open to ways God may be using this crisis as a catalyst to encourage greater maturing. Growth usually does not occur during charmed stretches of life free of crises. When troubles mount, we grow by turning crises into occasions to plumb more deeply the resources of each phase of the Christian life.

A chief means of maturing is growth in the skills of prayer. The pastor should regularly offer guidance for the practice of prayer in sermons and in adult education courses. This encourages parishioners to make appointments to talk about prayer and sets the state for conversations about prayer during pastoral calls. Prayer is so clearly a phase related in the process of Christian maturing that it serves as an index of the parishioner's progress. To ask about someone's prayer life is to take one of the vital signs of the Christian life. There is a growing body of contemporary literature on prayer and the spiritual life. Kenneth Leech's *Soul Friend* is a good place to begin.

By natural extension parishioners will need to become conscious of their own party prejudices borrowed from parents in faith and contract for maturing as in part growing beyond them. This concern for the principal nurturing figures in the parishioner's life leads us to the place of psychic history in the story of a faith journey.

Along with conveying modes of faith by teaching and example, parenting figures in faith also convey the emotional states and the interaction with the self which they bonded to their modes of faith. If in certain particulars, the parents' partaking of grace felt like the eating of sour grapes, their children's teeth will be set on edge when the children experience the same particulars of grace. Just as there are no parenting figures who were so perfect that they did not burden us as they nurtured us, so there are no nurturing figures in faith who did not also fasten on us modes of relating to God, to ourselves, and to others that are distortions of the good news of God's attempts to nurture us. Pastoring people toward maturing in the Christian life cannot simply replace psychological counseling. When our attempts to mature as Christians run into obsessive guilt and shameful or angry impatience with ourselves, we need to sort out the way God wants to deal with us from the way we are dealing with ourselves out of our psychic history. When the bad news of our psychic conditioning threatens to overwhelm the good news of God's grace, psychological counseling may be in order to help clear the ground for a less encumbered appreciation of the gospel.

At this point the work of therapist and of prophetic guide complement each other. The prophetic guide offers the grace of God in the fresh space that psychic awareness and strength open up. It is not appropriate simply to hand the parishioner over to the therapist until the psychological work is done. In that case therapy replaces spiritual direction. The therapist and the pastor need to work simultaneously. There is an analogy in one of the Gospels. The therapist engages in exorcism, while the pastor offers experiences of the Holy Spirit to fill the void left by each departing spirit, lest "seven other spirits more evil . . . enter and dwell there; and the last state of that man become worse than the first" (Luke 11:26). The point is to avoid substituting therapy's experience of the self at depth for the use of the means of grace and the concomitant experience of God at depth. At the same time we must allow therapy to make its contribution by disentangling the self from unfortunate patterns of human parenting that are being confused with the parenting of God. For parishioners with heavy psychological baggage, maturing in the Christian life may be interpreted as the increasing ascendancy of God's nurturing in the Holy Spirit over the nurturing we have received at the hands of other human beings. For this process to work, the therapist and the pastor will need to sympathize enough with each other's goals and procedures to allow their mutual efforts to be complementary rather than competitive. To recommend this therapeutic procedure to parishioners, the pastor will need to be able to recognize those cases where psychohistory seems to be overwhelming the gospel story.

Knowing the distinctive function of the guide as pastor delivers the minister from being a cheap therapist-in-residence to the congregation. A great spiritual guide once notified his charges that if any persons wished to make doing the whole will of God the aim of their lives, he would be willing to counsel with them as long and as often as they liked. Otherwise he was not available. Perhaps the guide as pastor will want to be less abrupt about it, but this does point in the direction the ministry needs to go after decades of wandering after therapists in search of our true function as pastors.

Concern for the parishioner's psychological story is important for guidance toward spiritual maturing not only when it presents obstacles but also when it unfolds normally. The predictable stages and transitions of adult development with their tasks, crises, and opportunities become major occasions for maturing in the Christian life. The Christian life becomes incarnate in the psychosocial development of adult life as it is now being described by people like Levinson for men and Sheehy for women.[69]

Bringing the pattern for maturing in the Christian life to bear on each stage and transition of the adult life cycle provides the connection with lived experience that makes the gospel exciting and helpful to a congregation.

It is safe to say that for the next decade this exploration of the connection between phases of the Christian life and the adult life cycle will be the most fruitful avenue for relevance of the gospel to personal life. The amazing uniformity of pattern in American adult development that we see emerging from psychosocial research reveals a cultural fate that is fastening itself on American adults with all the implacable tyranny of the astral gods and goddesses of Hellenistic religion in the period of the New Testament. Salvation, then as now, includes liberation from this merciless personal fate to gospel freedom to be fully human. As pastors take personal histories they will need to gather the information about psychosocial development as a context for spiritual maturing.

A major key to the capacity to draw gospel implications for adult life stages will depend on the clergyperson's own awareness of his or her own negotiation of the path of adulthood. In a beginning way David Giles and I have worked out a pattern of classical development by using a Levinson framework to organize our experience with a group of male clergy. David worked as a district superintendent and I as a teacher of continuing education. Our findings suggest that unless we begin applying greater Christian maturing to clerical careers, clergy are in for the same sad fate we see overtaking other middle-class working males in America. Clergy need to pioneer the shaping of Christian maturing for our time in the laboratory of their own careers. We are much more like our parishioners than they suppose. Out of the pressure cooker of clerical careers may come a fresh announcement of the nearness of the kingdom of God to workingpeople that is fully as arresting as Jesus' announcement to his contemporaries.

For clergy to become skilled spiritual guides they will need to band together for mutual guidance until a generation of spiritual directors for Protestant clergy emerges out of their explorations together. As we have already noted, clergy need soma groups just as badly as do laity. They especially need groups where they practice spiritual discernment and guidance with one another until the ancient art becomes comfortably familiar again.

Prophetic Guide to Mission in Community to Communities

In order to mature, each parish member needs to be engaged with others in mission. That means groups of parishioners with approximately the same phase engagement gathering as combination mission-support groups. The mission agenda for every group is set in broad outline by the triple requirements of witness, charity, and justice. Groups should be led to choose individual and collective targets for mission on all three fronts. We have already discussed this targeting as the missionary focus of a soma group.

Just as soma groups mount their mission as a community they should be encouraged to see their targets as communities. The transformation of individuals and the liberation of communities go hand in hand. But the level at which groups can imagine transformation and liberation will depend on their own location within the phases of Christian maturing. As a general rule, mission-support groups will fall into two types—disciple groups and soma groups. Each group's ability to witness, offer charity, and act for justice will be tied to its dominant phase of consciousness.

In both groups one ongoing task will be to clarify each person's story as witness to the truth and blessedness of the gospel. Among people who are predominantly in a disciple phase the emphasis will lie in the satisfactions that come in knowing the meaning of life, in having definite guidelines for the living out of that meaning, and in enjoying God's material support. Practice in telling and hearing each other has the effect of improving their ability to explain the difference that being a Christian makes in their lives. This amounts to training for witness. The Lord's Prayer makes a good outline of the points of doctrine and experience that beginning witnesses should be comfortable discussing.

Those conscious of the operation of the Spirit in their lives might practice telling their faith stories with a slightly different emphasis. These stories will include examples of personal transformation and the joy of intimacy with God they experience in the practice of the presence of God. The emphasis of witness among the more mature will likely lie on the beauty of the relationship with the Godhead themselves rather than, as in discipleship, upon meeting felt needs. The more mature will want to report the redefining of their needs as God's nurture of them unfolds. To explain the gift that the Godhead are in themselves, the more mature need to develop some ability to describe the Trinity and the role each of the three persons in it plays in the ongoing experience of transformation and maturing. Greater familiarity with God at work as Trinity increases the capacity to cooperate in the mission that the Godhead are already constantly pursuing.

On the front of developing works of charity, the adage applies that charity begins at home. People who are concentrated in the discipleship phase will find it easier to note the needs of people close to home and in similar life circumstances, i.e., people with whom they can easily identify. Offers to help meet these needs will come out of abundance and surplus rather than from the sharing of goods, time, and energy which might detract from their own standard of living. More mature Christians share from their own substance (Mark 12:43–44) with the effect of real redistribution of the level of well-being (II Cor. 8:13–15). As people mature they come to care about those who are remote in terms of class, economic status, race, and geography.

All of this implies that the pastoral and educational resources of the parish need to be mobilized to expand parish consciousness to include ever-widening concentric circles of communities. Concern begins at the parish level but moves progressively through state, region, and nation to global village.

Denomination, National Council of Churches, World Council of Churches, and many other church agencies, will offer suggestions of pressing needs. Emphasis ought to lie on the prayerful, Spirit-generated agenda to which each task-support group senses that it is being led. I judge that the greatest short circuit in the whole hookup of denominational and world church agitation for charitable mission lies in the failure to provide for the process of forming a convictional consensus on the part of church groups so that they own particular projects as *their* God-given task and opportunity. The needs of the world are overwhelming. We need the Spirit's help in identifying our own special responsibility.

The same applies to issues of justice. At this point the guide is most clearly prophetic. Individuals and groups need to study, pray, discuss, and wait upon God until they sense they are being led in their analysis of the concentric circles of community to the particular concern for justice to which God is calling them as a group and as individuals. The devoted life completes itself when some "concern" for justice fastens itself upon budding saints, individually and in groups. Periodic denominational mission emphases need to be seen as suggestions that God takes and applies to the hearts and lives of individuals and groups who then commit themselves to one or a few of them.

Perhaps no other facet of mission is tied so closely to the level of Christian maturing as action for social justice. Parishioners predominantly in the discipleship phase will be committed mainly to the adjustment of familiar systems. They tend to equate the systemic arrangements in which they have achieved or hope to achieve material well-being, status, and influence with the kingdom of God. The original disciples of Jesus equated the kingdom of God with their dreams of a powerful, affluent, independent Israel. The discipleship phase tends to define acts of justice in terms of enforcing the prevailing system. Typical of this approach are the activities of Nader's organization, Common Cause, legal aid for the poor, Chavez' organization of farm workers, the enforcing of civil rights, legislation for minority groups, and revival and application of the doctrine of just war to international conflict. Much of the motivation for this form of action for justice depends on hope for success in achieving the declared goals within a foreseeable time span.

Acts of justice on the part of the more mature arise out of a consciousness that has come to distinguish the level of justice envisaged by all prevailing systemic arrangements from the fuller justice that God intends. Sharing this more radical vision of divine justice will inspire Christians to imagine changes in existing systems, new systems, and alternative systems alongside prevailing ones that move to a level of justice beyond the dreams of the designers and keepers of the status quo. Familiar examples of such action would include the advocacy of social services aimed at the redistribution of material well-being so that there would be some agreed-upon level of affluence for all, including refusal to live above this parity level, unilateral disarmament, pacifism, nonviolent refusal to abide by existing laws that perpetuate injustice with the willingness to suffer the penalties that existing laws demand. Agitation for such interpretations of justice must be motivated more by the vision of the eschatological, future kingdom of God than by hope of success under the circumstances of this world. There is little that is new here. The novelty we seek is increasing support from a majority of members because they are maturing spiritually.

The historic tension between evangelical and social activist obscures the connection between witness and justice which must be woven into one whole tapestry of faithfulness. Only when people are evangelized to the point of transformed consciousness is there a popular sympathy for root changes in social justice, let alone the will to act to implement them.

Charity understood as relief of a particular need until new social systems can eliminate that need altogether becomes even more crucial when envisioned radical change of social arrangements is not likely to happen in the foreseeable future, let alone in the lifetime of those who care and are cared for. In the discipleship phase, when the system is trusted and modifications to it are within reach, charity seems temporary. When hopes and dreams of justice expand, charity never ends.

I have called groups with these concerns mission-support groups because once mission projects are targeted and action has begun, the groups will need to supply the support necessary to help people stay with their project when resistance to change comes, as it surely must. Injustice continues because it is to someone's advantage. Beneficiaries of the status quo see agitators for greater justice as a clear and present danger to their own just deserts. Some equivalent of persecution is bound to come. Parishioners will only continue in the face of this resistance when the church community provides them support, encouragement, reward, and affirmation to match the threats of opponents. The doctrine of the church as the body of Christ declares that human life is primarily social and not individualistic. It is unreal to ask individuals to tackle the communities of the world for mission. Then there is no contest. Mission must always be the church engaging the world and individual Christians only as members of the church. So clerical leaders as guides to community-in-mission must be skillful at developing group processes that maintain high morale in the face of pressure to cease and desist from the action for justice that these groups devise.

Acts of charity and justice provide natural occasions for witness. When opportunities are sought out to help others with no expectation of reward in return, it is natural for unchurched partners in and recipients of charity and justice to wonder aloud why this is being done. That wondering constitutes an invitation to witness to the blessings of discipleship.

But the witnessing Christian must not always wait to be asked, any more than the charitable or justice-seeking Christian waits for an invitation for these ministries. Analysis of every level of community, from hometown to global village, targets the unchurched and vaguely churched with as much intention to remedy their deprivation and oppression as do strategies of relief and liberation. Jesus is the model. He went to the crowds with healing and also with an invitation to accept the reign of God by making a personal commitment to follow him. That was the meaning of the saying, "Take my yoke upon you and learn from me; for I am gentle and lowly in heart, and you will find rest for your souls" (Matt. 11:29). The ultimate deprivation and oppression is estrangement from the God who pleads with us through this invitation of Jesus. So faithful disciples canvass the world near and far for those who do not yet enjoy the sustenance and liberation of Christian discipleship in order to invite them to it. It is a grotesque development of modern Christianity that it ever supposed that life could be satisfying or complete without discipleship. It is a romantic heresy to suppose that once the poor and the oppressed are ministered to with charity and justice, we in the church have done as much for them as God could wish. Likewise it is heresy to suppose that the affluent and those who have more than their fair share of power and status in society deserve to be ignored or blamed for their circumstances to the extent that the church makes them no offer of grace since they already enjoy so many of the other good things of life. All Christians in mission with integrity naturally begin and end with the firm conviction that entrance to and growth in the Christian life is the "pearl of great price." If one had to choose among the benefits of charity, justice, and discipleship, the wise person would trade the other two for discipleship. Fortunately, the great tradition of the church never contemplated forcing such a decision upon its neighbors. That has waited for the outrageous development of modern party Protestantism, split into evangelistic and social action Christians.

The Guide as Educator

The congregation's engagement in mission just described assumes a fairly sophisticated analysis of culture from the point of view of justice. It also assumes that charity, justice, and accompanying witness are grounded in some understanding and experience of the gospel that are transforming consciousness, generating care, and encouraging action. What this implies is that each congregation must mount the equivalent of a seminary theological education geared to the functioning of laity. The only things to exclude from professional theological education are the preparations to preach, arrange liturgies, administer the sacraments, and fill the role of institutional leader as each denomination defines that role. Most of theological education remains as a responsibility of congregational life. Next to the role of prophetic guide to justice in community, no role is so neglected by clergy as prophetic guide to education. Laity seldom expect the minister to be their theological educator, yet no ministry with integrity can be carried out by laity without this service. Failure to act as direct teacher and dean or principal of a school of discipleship by its pastoral leader probably accounts more than any other single factor for a congregation's inability to mature in its ministry.

It helps to approach the educational task with the question: What are the elements that ground ministry with integrity? They include:

1. An intellectual base: i.e., a theological stance, articulate and consciously connected to Scripture and tradition, that informs the practice of ministry.

2. An experiential base: i.e., regular and lively use of the means of grace (particularly meditative prayer) that issues in a conscious experience of the presence of God blessing, leading, and empowering the journey of faith.

3. Readiness for evangelism: i.e., clarity about the story of one's own beginning and progress in the Christian life, and the ability to tell it so that it connects with the life and faith experience of the listener.

4. Readiness for charity and justice: an analytic perspective on contemporary culture that provides a context for sensing and meeting the most pressing needs for charity and justice at home and abroad.

5. A theory of the Christian life that provides a reference for understanding one's own faith journey, adapting the means of grace to resource it, and to aid others in entering and negotiating that same journey. The aim here is to prepare to utilize and to aid the master function of the minister as prophetic guide.

6. An appreciation of the character of a voluntary institution as a vehicle of the life of the church and a willingness to learn how the particular congregation and denomination are organized for nurture and mission so that they may accept responsibility for making these institutions work to these ends.

All of the above need to be taught to adults even though Sunday church school curricula may have touched on some of the items in childhood. Adults need to apply already familiar curriculum materials to their lives as adults.

By engaging directly in teaching and in planning the complete educational strategy of the congregation's life, the pastoral leader models the importance of education. Only so will education receive the emphasis it requires and provide the base for a congregation's maturing in the Christian life. The principal thing the guide as educator needs to teach is that his or her master role as prophetic guide to maturing in the Christian life corresponds with the master function of the congregation. The vision of a congregation maturing in nurture and in mission should motivate, shape, and permeate every congregational function. This vision needs to be communicated to the leadership first of all and then to every person planning, supporting, or teaching in the educational program. One of the great fallacies in the educational life of congregations is the assumption that because laypersons are willing to serve in leadership or teaching capacities, they know what they are doing if they are managing somehow to function. Denominations make the same mistake when they appoint college students to be leaders of congregations. They may operate successfully so far as congregational expectations are concerned, but they have no chance to minister with integrity, given their lack of preparation. What is worse, should they decide to enter seminary, they are skeptical of the value of the education offered there, since they have been lulled by experience into supposing they know how to do ministry already. The obvious result is that without adequate preparation and experience they tend to freeze themselves and those to whom they minister at the level of their own immaturity.

Often congregations hope to organize parish life for success, either at crowd or at discipleship levels. This forecloses further maturing. For example, once a congregation has learned to raise its budget by having dinners, bazaars, and raffles, buttressed perhaps by the windfall of an endowment fund for operating expenses, it loses the capacity to understand stewardship as an expression of maturing in Spirit and in mission. The primary aim of the pastor as educator is to create a cadre of leaders committed to the vision of a congregation maturing in the Christian life who eventually fill the offices of leadership on the organizational chart of the congregation. Especially in the beginning of a pastoral relationship the pastor personally will need to teach each of the <u>six areas</u> that ground integrity until he or she has conveyed the vision to a cadre of teachers who then share their learning with others.

cf. 161–62

As the congregation matures, the pastoral leader may withdraw from much of the direct teaching but will need to continue to supervise teachers in terms of vision. The guide as educator must monitor the enterprise to ensure that subject matter and method in each area are appropriate to the goal of a congregation maturing in the Christian life. The pastoral leader will always need to teach in learning groups geared to discipleship because the authority that the clerical leader bears at this stage cannot be duplicated by another member of the congregation.

To begin with, the format may well be structured programs with concentration on subject matter. As parishioners mature, the format moves toward workshop and support groups of peer teacher-learners where experience and subject matter interweave, until finally the workshop is displaced by the soma group where a given set of people engage simultaneously in learning, teaching, nurture, worship, and mission. Such soma groups then set the ethos of the congregation where every member is invited in accord with the timetable of his or her own maturing, to participate in all the functions of such a soma group.

I suspect that of the six areas for integrity in mission, the one involving a conscious experience of the presence of God has been taught least in mainline Protestant congregations. We are mostly oriented to service and everyday consciousness. We are more in tune with the secular world of the workplace than with the tradition of meditative prayer and the practice of the presence of God in closet, home, and workplace. Beside preaching, explicit instruction in prayer by the pastoral leader best acquaints parishioners with the master vision of the life of the congregation as a corporate journey toward maturing in the Christian life. Meeting the pastor as teacher and preacher of prayer invites parishioners to seek him or her out as a guide to maturing in the Christian life.

I realize that, to begin with, most Protestant clergy will feel they are only posing as spiritual guides, since most of

them were never trained for that function. To offer ourselves to others as a guide does not mean we declare ourselves qualified to be one. We ought to admit candidly that
we are only learning how to be guides and will only do
what we can. Getting on with the task is the major way to
become qualified—this and finding a guide of your own.

One of the great guides in the tradition of spiritual direction was not ashamed to declare himself unqualified as
a guide even as he sought to help in just that way. Francis
de Sales wrote in the preface to his classic, *Introduction to
the Devout Life:* "It is true, my dear reader, that I write
about the devout life although I myself am not devout. Yet
it is certainly not without a desire of becoming so and it
is such affection that encourages me to instruct you. . . . To
study is a good way to learn; to hear is a still better way;
to teach is the best of all. 'It often happens' says St. Augustine, 'that the office of giving gives us the merit to receive,
and the office of teaching serves as a foundation for learning' "[70] We need not be wholly self-taught. Opportunities
for continuing education in spiritual guidance begin to
abound.

Finally, education that issues in maturing in mission for
laity must have its own equivalent of the professional side
of theological education. Theological seminaries teach
polity and procedures for executing mission on the clergyperson's work site. Lay theological education should teach
polity and procedures for mission for laypersons on their
work sites. The other major context in which laity carry
out their call to mission is the family. We need to foster a
sense in the church that the polity and skills of workplace
and family finally take precedence over the polity and
skills that serve the church as institution. Failing that, we
rob the laity of their full participation in ministry as surely
as if we maintained that only clergy have a calling to be
ministers. Most clergy would declare that the ministry of
the church to the world belongs mainly to the laity, but

our resourcing denies it. We leave vocational guidance
and ethics of the work site to others, thereby depriving
laity of the tools they need most to turn their work into an
expression of mission.

In past centuries, when Protestantism was healthier,
laity were entitled to a calling as surely as were clergy. The
church provided a body of ethical guidance adapted to
their callings in the world. We must recover the tradition
of a Christian ethic of work in order for work to become
the occasion for growth in grace that it once was. Accordingly, the church owes to the laity a training in ministerial
skill at work as surely as seminaries provide clergy with
skills in preaching or administering a congregation. Only
when we bring work into the educational design of the
parish will we signal that being Christian means drawing
work into the orbit of the faith journey. As things stand,
parishioners are condemned to lead double lives—one at
church and home and the other at work. When we equip
laity for their callings, the mission of the church as the
body of Christ will again have the chance to go forward
where it was intended—in the world that laity inhabit
every working day. Although we avoid thinking of it this
way, our concentration of churchly activity within the
institutional framework of congregations amounts to monastic withdrawal and the gnosticizing of the gospel.

Because of the feminization of education in the
churches, we offer more help for the vocation of parenting
than we do for work as a vocation. However, parents need
a clearer understanding of the faith journey that Christian
parenting is designed to serve. We have relatively great
skill and experience in relating the tradition of the church
to the development of the child in families. We need to
work out more clearly how much of the faith journey can
be negotiated only as adults. We are beginning to see how
exciting the faith journey can be when correlated with
stages and transitions of adulthood. Our first order of busi-

ness for parenting and families ought to be to hammer out a gospel context for the transition to adulthood, adolescence and young adulthood, comparable to the one we are developing for the mid-life crisis. This is not to imply that adolescence has not been carefully studied by Christian educators, but we have not conveyed to parents how this most difficult time for parenting may become a great occasion for maturing in the Christian life. Our theory of the Christian life has not kept pace with our theories of psychosocial development. I am afraid now that most parish parents are content with their parenting if their children move smoothly to acquire the manners and education necessary for upward mobility. Our vision of maturing in the Christian life implies that upward mobility as middle-class achievers ought to take second place to the project of becoming upwardly mobile in terms of maturing in faith. Parents are better at equipping their children to grow up achievers than they are at equipping them to grow up Christian. A biblical theological version of faith development makes possible a renewed impetus for specifically Christian parenting.

The Guide as Administrator

Voluntary organizations distinguish themselves from other organizations by not paying their participants. Voluntary organizations depend on vision to fuel the enterprise. Paying organizations manage by setting objectives that money can buy. In voluntary organizations, vision is what motivates; the fundamental management procedure must be management by vision rather than by objective. Of course the vision of a congregation maturing in the Christian life implies many particular objectives. The pastoral leader as administrator does aid the organization by helping to set objectives for each arm of the operation, but his or her chief contribution will be to insist that every long-range or short-range objective has a clear connection with the overarching vision. Thus the distinguishing technique of the guide as administrator is management by vision.

The vision of a congregation maturing in the Christian life implies a multilevel organization that services the needs of the various phases of maturing in the Christian life. The twofold objective of the parish organization founded on the vision of maturing is, first, to draw people to enter the journey of the Christian life and, second, to offer resources for each phase of maturing. These two objectives imply two kinds of gatherings for which there must be administrative planning and support. Following the example of the Gospels, we may designate those interested in benefiting from the ministries of the church but not yet committed to following Jesus as "crowd." Jesus' ministry began with crowd functions that appealed to the interests and felt needs of people, *but always with the invitation to discipleship present in some form.*

Church picnics, dinners, parties, campouts, and other social functions might fall into this category. These events appeal to the unaffiliated or inactive because they are so closely tied to parallel celebrations in the culture. They require little or no Christian commitment to understand and enjoy. These should be administered along with other evangelism programs with an eye to being as appealing as possible to outsiders *and should always be accompanied by some form of invitation to discipleship.*

While caring is the base that underlies all these expressions, the form of these crowd events relates most directly to media theater. The guide as administrator of crowd events is an impresario of happenings designed to stimulate interest in discipleship. I do not mean that a happening must involve large numbers to be a crowd event. An intimate small group in a member's home can be a crowd happening, if it appeals to "crowd" types and becomes an occasion for stimulating interest in discipleship.

Sunday morning worship is partly a crowd event in the sense that it should contain elements that appeal to felt needs of the uncommitted, but it is so multifaceted that it defies classification. When it is done well, it ministers to every level of Christian maturing as well as to crowd interests. Because it requires no preparation and a minimum of spontaneous and gifted participation, I would classify Sunday worship as a discipleship event primarily, in the sense that the clerical leader as preacher-liturgist provides the script to which the worshiper need only respond. Indeed, any other form of participation would disrupt most orders of worship! Sunday worship is a crowd event also in that some come just to observe. No one monitors their following along. They need not sing or recite the confession or read responses if they choose not to. But because the order is for those who are following Christ, discipleship is its focus. But in the measure to which it is a crowd event, it should always contain some form of invitation to discipleship.

Sunday worship is also an event for those making a transition to life in the Spirit, since the trinitarian liturgy invites and provides for an explicit experience of the presence of the Godhead in the Spirit. Lest events primarily geared for discipleship tend to convey the idea that discipleship is the only phase of maturing in faith, every worship service should also contain some form of invitation to life in the Spirit.

Sunday worship is also an event for soma group members and missioners because it speaks to God, allows God to speak, and listens to God in ways that only those with greater maturing appreciate. Sunday morning worship, then, should be administered as an event that nurtures simultaneously every phase of the faith journey. The genius of this parish-wide event is that it does encompass the whole journey of faith. It thereby binds the whole congregation together in one community, celebrating the common journey of all, regardless of their dominant phase of maturing at the time.

The Sunday morning worship service reminds us of the simultaneous juxtaposition of all the phases of the Christian life. The same order of worship ministers to them all simultaneously. Most Christians experience some aspect of all three phases simultaneously. But at any one time particular Christians need to emphasize one phase over others in order to nurture their maturing. It is this emphasis which the administrator hopes to serve in the spectrum of congregational gatherings we are reviewing.

Maturing parishioners must be drawn into other gatherings beyond Sunday morning common worship. We have spoken already of disciple groups and soma groups or mission-support groups. All these are necessary to take a congregation through the full range of resources that lead to continuing maturing.

The point I wish to make here is that the guide as administrator must be very intentional about structuring the life of the congregation beyond the Sunday morning worship service. In most parishes all other congregational functions beyond the traditional worship service taper off in significance. It is customary to measure the strength of a congregation's life by how many people attend Sunday worship in proportion to the total membership. A better measure of the strength of a congregation as a vehicle for maturing would be the number and proportion of the adult membership that meet in groups—disciple schooling, soma, and mission-support—outside the sanctuary at other times of the week. A maturing congregation will be one that relocates the center of gravity of its life from Sunday morning worship to the groups that express life in the Spirit and the church as the body of Christ in nurture and in mission. This relocation of emphasis represents the same move the early church made with respect to its location within the larger administrative unit of Judaism. It is the move from Temple back to tent.

From Temple to Tents

In the time of Jesus and the early church the emphasis in Judaism's life had come to be concentrated in the elaborate worship rites of the Temple in Jerusalem. The Temple was Judaism's central religious institution and the rallying point for all Jews regardless of sect or location. It was the judgment of Jesus in the Temple-cleansing incident that the Temple had come to be a distraction and an obstacle to Judaism's God-intended mission to be a blessing to all the families of the earth (Gen. 12:3). As a marketplace for sacrificial animals and as a national bank, its economic function had overwhelmed its proper function as a base for world mission.[71] "Is it not written, 'My house shall be called a house of prayer for all the nations?' But you have made it a den of robbers" (Mark 11:17). The early church concluded that Jesus' estimate of the Temple was confirmed by God in the rending of the curtain of the Temple from top to bottom, exposing the Holy of Holies shorn of the presence of God. God's presence had moved to the midst of the church on the road in mission.

In the experience of the early church the Temple turned out to have inhibited the missionary purpose of the people of God rather than facilitate it. I judge that the concentration of emphasis in the life of most parishes upon the Sunday morning worship in a sanctuary designed exclusively for that purpose tends to have the same effect upon the people of God unless that worship is administered in the context of a developmental understanding of Christian faith. The history of the origin of Israel's Temple helps to explain why sanctuaries tend to arrest the missionary movement of God's people.

The author of II Samuel presented the project of building a temple for Yahweh as an extension of David's own upward mobility. King Hiram of Tyre recognized David's rise to prominence as king of Israel and conqueror of Jerusalem by the gift of a custom-built house of cedar (II Sam. 5:11–12). Once David settled down in this fine home he felt it inappropriate that the Lord's Ark should be housed in something so déclassé as a tent (II Sam. 7:1–3). That night the word of the Lord to Nathan explained that the Lord felt no need for a house of cedar, that a tent had been good enough from the beginning. In other words God found it a pretentious idea. The Lord gave reluctant permission to David's son to build. After the festival of dedication, the Lord appeared to Solomon and warned him that anytime Israel faltered in their devotion to the Lord, the Temple would become "a heap of ruins" (I Kings 9:8). That fate was fulfilled in the destruction of Solomon's Temple in 587 B.C. and its successor in A.D. 70. "Do you see these great buildings? There will not be left here one stone upon another, that will not be thrown down" (Mark 13:2). Upon the failure of the Temple, the early church in effect returned to tents, for "Christianity had no identifiable places of assembly for at least two hundred years."[72] The early church was a house church, expending its resources on love and mission rather than on special housing for itself. The Godhead were again housing themselves in tents, living tents of congregations indwelt by the Spirit.

The point is clear. As administrators we need to imagine meetingplaces for the people of God that dramatize their location in mission or on the way to mission, not settled down somewhere congratulating themselves on how far they have come up in the world. Failing that, we may find ourselves huddled in sanctuaries whose curtains have long since hung in shreds, exposing the empty space where Yahweh used to dwell. How many clergy there are who secretly wish their elaborate and costly-to-maintain sanctuaries would burn to the ground so their congregations could begin again more modestly!

But some equivalent to the destruction of Jerusalem is no answer to what has often been called the church's "edifice complex." The answer is to administer a variety of levels of church life: one that naturally emphasizes the building for crowd and discipleship purposes and other levels on the way to and on location in mission.

The administrator of a program for a faith journey that unfolds in phases must be committed to a split-level church or churches within a church. It is true that most congregations already have enough groups and committees to occupy the pastoral leader on every available evening. Where will time and energy come from to add another whole set? What will parishioners think who find themselves in groups where curricula and agenda imply an early phase of maturing? Will they not become jealous of those who seem to rank higher? John Wesley's use of the Methodist class meetings within the Anglican Church offers a model. All who are willing to make the commitment involved and to abide by the participatory responsibilities are welcome to the soma mission groups. The groups do not exclude people. People exclude themselves!

What will become of the institutional standing committees if everyone starts going to other meetings? Wesley emphasized that those who attended class meetings had a higher level of responsibility to the congregation as institution than those who chose not to join the classes. Thus class members outgave, outcommuned, outattended, and outsupported the common institution to which their sister and brother Anglicans were committed. Gathering must never seem exclusive. Groups must periodically open themselves to newcomers who wish to commit to the contract for the maturing of that group. Meanwhile Sunday morning worship always continues for the whole congregation.

The answer to the extra time and energy demanded of the guide is that as parishioners mature they grow to the point of sharing the ministry which the pastoral leader has heretofore carried mostly alone. As maturing laity emerge to share the work of administration, the guide will eventually have less to do rather than more.

The final administrative function of the guide is to devise a system, perhaps in combination with the one by which stories of faith journeys are taken, to keep some updated inventory of the gifts and graces of each parishioner. The whole structure of congregational life needs to offer each parishioner an opportunity to contribute to nurture and mission, thereby sharing in the ministry of the whole congregation to itself and to others.

Our sketch of the journey of maturing in the Christian life has displayed the amazing extent to which maturing laity are capable of sharing the work of the ministry. The obvious answer to the time and energy required to interview members for faith histories and to inventory the congregation for gifts and graces is to train a cadre of lay interviewers with a standardized interview schedule and record-keeping procedure. This could inaugurate training of lay spiritual guides.

The result envisioned by all of these suggestions for the guide as administrator is not to burden the administrator further but to multiply many times over the ministry which the clergyperson now attempts to carry on alone. Congregational administration is virtually a solo ministry. The administrator-guide may become, with strong congregational maturing, the companion overseer of the ministries of many.

The vision of a congregation maturing in the Christian life offers the best chance I see of clergy being delivered from the impossibly hectic and forever unfinished round to which the profession now threatens to condemn every pastoral leader except those few who have large staffs.

Even with large staffs senior pastors often find that the hassle multiplies in proportion to the number of staff, since the senior person must always compensate for the staff's immaturity.

Conclusion

I hope I have shown how a biblical theological theory of the Christian life provides a rationale to move in the direction to which we are all in principle committed, namely, to make ministry a function of the whole congregation and not just of the clergy. Clergy who attempt the master role of prophetic guide allow that possibility to emerge. With God the Father setting the pace and God the Spirit enabling as we go, the church in its local congregational expression can become the body of the Son whose full ministry continues to unfold in the congregation's midst, not as our doing, but as Theirs. When that begins to happen, clergy will have space to receive another "compleat angler's" final benediction "upon all that are lovers of virtue, and dare trust in his providence, and be quiet, and go a-angling." The ministry may yet be as much fun as fishing. Meanwhile: "Study to be quiet" (I Thess. 4:11).

APPENDIX I
FOOTNOTE ON TONGUES

With the essential components of the transition to Spirit in mind, we are in a position to evaluate speaking in tongues within the framework of the faith journey. It obviously cannot be *the* mark of the transition I am proposing, given the example of the Corinthian congregation. The Corinthians show that it was possible for one to speak in tongues and be concerned only with one's own spiritual experience regardless of the effect on others (I Cor. 13:1; 14:1–32). Speaking in tongues was a common mark of piety in Corinth (I Cor. 14:5). Probably some there who spoke in tongues thought themselves moved on occasion to curse Jesus (I Cor. 12:3). Among those who missed the significance of the elements of the Lord's Supper and caroused at table instead were, no doubt, some who spoke in tongues (I Cor. 11:20–34). Far from showing the signs of spiritual growth, many were ill and dying. The Corinthian congregation was riddled with factions and party spirit and was tolerant of incest, although most of congregation spoke in tongues (I Cor. 1:10–12; 3:1–9; 5:1–13; 11:19). For all these reasons, in a congregation famous for speaking in tongues, Paul had to rate Corinthian Christians as being highly immature, rank beginners, men and women "of the flesh," "babes in Christ," "children in their thinking" (I Cor. 3:1; 14:20). No doubt they considered themselves mature (II Cor. 10:1–13:14, especially 11:5 and 12:11). This tendency to confuse speaking in tongues with spiritual maturity, thus blocking real maturing, may have led Paul to omit speaking in tongues from his list of gifts for Rome (Rom. 12:6ff.). The Pauline school after him dropped it altogether (Eph. 4:7ff.). For the same reason the New Testament church outside of Paul either changed tongues to foreign languages (Luke) or dropped it altogether. In effect, it came to be included under Paul's warning that "Jews demand signs" (I Cor. 1:22). Speaking in tongues did not wear well in the early church.

Nevertheless speaking in tongues may serve maturing if it stays within the kind of prayer that belongs to the transition that Chapter 3 has been describing. The warning raised by Corinthian piety is that a person can have striking manifestations of the Spirit and still be so possessed by disciplelike illusions that these manifestations do not work toward maturing. In the religiosity of Hellenistic culture there was a world-denying, gnostic kind of piety that scholars equate with the so-called "divine man" that was in its own way just as illusory and immature as the nationalist warrior piety of Palestinian Judaism.

In the context of Hellenistic religiosity I find the positive significance of speaking in tongues in its ability to answer to the feeling of estrangement from God so characteristic of Hellenistic culture. Gnosticism witnessed to the fact that many in the Hellenistic world felt that they were at a terrifying distance from God. Separated from God by many-layered barriers of heavens, the Hellenist felt caught in a situation similar to that of an abandoned, unloved, and emotionally deprived child with marvelous but remote parents. To such religious waifs, tongues represented a return of those marvelous parents to take the child back into the stream of nurturing love.

In Palestinian terms "tongues" meant special and powerful equipment to continue a prophetic ministry promised in the Old Testament and modeled by Jesus. This Spirit presence gave continuing meaning to Jesus' promise of the drawing near of the kingdom of God. The important difference of course is that in the experience of tongues there is no figure of Jesus giving form and content to the coming kingdom, so that the subjectivity of the early charismatic had little to guide it. The eccentric piety of the Corinthians was the result. Hellenistic subjectivity could simply displace any distinctive Christian content, as the cursing of Jesus showed (I Cor. 12:1–3).

For those who speak in tongues everything depends on what happens when the road of the faith journey turns toward the cross and the crucial transition it announces. The cross was as much a stumbling block to the Corinthians' ecstatic spirituality as it had been to the original Palestinian disciples' holy politics (I Cor. 1:22). Present-day charismatics are right in their insistence that there is an important transition in the Christian life connected with an experience of the Spirit. They mislead, however, when they make speaking in tongues the unmistakable mark of this transition.

A Corinthian-like experience of speaking in tongues no more guarantees a maturing life of faith than did the response of the four fishermen to Jesus' call to discipleship. Only when the gift of tongues accompanies the dispelling of illusions and misunderstanding about God's reign does it represent a transition to life in the Spirit. The gift of tongues can as easily confirm illusion and misconception as mark their passing.

This note on tongues implies two useful rules for pastoral leaders. One, parishioners who insist that speaking in tongues is necessary to spiritual maturing should be encouraged to join a Pentecostal church. They disqualify themselves for membership in the mainline denominations. A second rule emerges from Paul's guidelines for the Corinthian congregation. No meetings should be permitted in which people speak in tongues en masse. That is to misunderstand the story of Pentecost. Speaking in tongues is essentially a means of private devotion. It may occasionally appear in gatherings where two or three at most speak and then only when there is an interpreter for each (I Cor. 14:27–28). The early church survived its charismatic movements by following this advice. We are well advised to follow suit.

Appendix II
FAITH HISTORY INTERVIEW

Orientation Comments

In its own way an interview on faith history is something like the history a family physician takes of a new patient. Knowing a patient's medical history makes it possible for the physician to plan for the continuing good health of the patient, to fend off predictable episodes of illness and to care more effectively when illness does come. Perhaps the major difference between a medical history and a faith history is that a faith history is oriented more to the healthy times than to the times of crisis. Indeed, most people find that talking about their pilgrimages and their beliefs as Christians is itself a means of grace that enhances and strengthens the faith they already have. I hope that will be true for you.

Besides enhancing your faith and giving me a chance to know you better, this interview has another purpose. In my continuing education for the ministry I need to gain skill and experience in understanding faith journeys. With your permission I may be reporting this interview to a group of clergy as part of our training. In this report I will not identify who you are. I will never divulge to anyone what we talk about together, for it will be a privileged communication between minister and parishioner. If at any time during our conversation you decide you would not like to continue or would not like me to report our conversation, we will stop. (Only use this paragraph if it applies.)

I ask your permission to record our conversation on tape. This will help me in making my notes. I will not duplicate the tape, nor play it for anyone else. When I have finished making my notes I will erase the tape.

Factual Data

Date and place of birth? Numbers and ages of brothers and sisters? Occupation of providing parent or parents? Ethnic and racial identification? Church affiliation? Own occupation? Marital status? Own family—their sexes and ages? Occupation of spouse?

Part I. Formative Figures

1. Were your parents religious? In what ways did they influence your faith formation as you were growing up?

2. Were there other adults who had an important influence on your religious nurture? Who were they and what influence did they have?

3. In your adult years what ministers, friends, teachers, or authors have had a special hand in shaping the faith you now hold? What were their contributions, both positive and negative?

4. Follow up on the influential figures to find out if they ever shared their own faith experiences. Did they pray, read Scripture, attend church, engage in ministry inside the institution or in mission outside the church in everyday life? Did their ministry inside or outside the church include evangelism, relief of people's needs, action or involvement for greater justice? In what ways?

A major function of Part I is to discover to what extent formative figures belong to evangelical or social action party types. Second, what marks did they show of the various phases of the Christian life?

Part II. Personal Journey

1. Was there a time when you consciously decided to become a Christian? What were the circumstances? Did any particular experiences of God lead up to or accompany this?

2. Have you ever had what might be called a conversion experience? If so, tell me about it.

3. Have you had or do you now have a continuing sense of the presence of God or of God's hand in your life?

4. What has been the best experience of God's activity in your life?

5. Was there ever a time when you felt let down by God?

6. Does God have a regular place in your everyday life? At home? At work or school?

7. When you come to look back on your life at its end in what ways do you hope most that it was an expression of faith?

8. In what way do you wish God would help you most in your life right now?

Part III. Particulars of Faith

1. Do you remember God having a hand in your choice of spouse?

2. If you are a parent, how do you hope to influence your family as a person of faith?

3. Do you remember God having a hand in your choice of occupation? In your occupation how do you hope that your faith makes a difference?

4. How does Jesus Christ help you in your relationship to God?

5. What would you choose as the most appropriate title or titles for Jesus—good man, prophet, teacher, Son of God, savior, Lord, Son of man? Why—what does it (they) mean to you?

6. Have you ever had any particular experiences of the Holy Spirit?

7. What do you think God most wants to accomplish in the world?

8. What has been your worst experience of the church?

9. What should the church be doing?

10. What has been your best experience of the church?

11. When you worship, what do you hope will happen?

12. What do you expect most from clergy?

13. Do you find the Sacraments of Baptism and the Lord's Supper particularly helpful?

14. What part does prayer play in your life? How often? When? What do you pray about? What happens as a result of your prayers?

15. Have you ever been part of a prayer group? What did it do?

16. How does serious illness or tragedy affect your relationship with God?

17. What does the Bible mean to you? What use do you make of it?

18. Are there any summaries or confessions of faith that especially express what you believe?

19. Would people who do not believe in Christ be better off if they did? Would you support efforts to help bring people to faith in Christ? Do you do anything yourself in regard to this?

20. Is racial injustice a faith issue for you? How do you express your concern?

21. How do you account for poverty from a religious point of view?

22. Should religion and politics have to do with each other? In what ways?

23. Do you think there are times when it is justified to disobey the law for religious reasons? Have you ever put yourself in such circumstances?

24. How do you think God feels about our nation?

25. What do you expect to happen to you when you come to die? Do you think faith will make a difference then?

26. How do you think you are doing as a Christian?

27. Do you have what used to be called a "besetting sin," some particular failing that keeps recurring? Do you find help from God to stay on top of it most of the time or does it win most of the time? [Do not ask to identify the failing. Leave it up to the parishioner to say or not.]

28. As you think back over your answers, are there any you are uneasy about? Would you like to add anything?

Thank you so much for your time and your candor. I cannot tell you how much it means for me to have the privilege of getting to know you in this way.

NOTES

1. James W. Fowler, *Stages of Faith: The Psychology of Human Development and the Quest for Meaning* (Harper & Row, 1981).

2. Jim Conway, *Men in Mid-Life Crisis* (David C. Cook Publishing Co., 1978), p. 57.

3. Edgar W. Mills and John P. Koval, *Stress in the Ministry* (New York: Ministry Studies Board and IDOC, 1971; 70 pp.), cited in Donald P. Smith, *Clergy in the Cross Fire: Coping with Role Conflicts in Ministry* (Westminster Press, 1973), p. 54.

4. David A. Giles and Neill Q. Hamilton, "Seasons of a Pastor's Life," *The Circuit Rider*, September 1980, p. 4.

5. H. Richard Niebuhr, *The Purpose of the Church and Its Ministry: Reflections on the Aims of Theological Education* (Harper & Brothers, 1956).

6. Donald P. Smith suggests "minister-director," "minister-executive," or "minister-manager," in *Clergy in the Cross Fire*, p. 153.

7. Samuel W. Blizzard, "The Protestant Parish Minister's Integrating Roles," *Religious Education*, Vol. 53, No. 4 (July–Aug. 1958), quoted in Smith, *Clergy in the Cross Fire*, p. 99.

8. David S. Schuller, Merton P. Strommen, and Milo L. Brekke, eds., *Ministry in America: A Complete Report and Analysis, Based on an In-Depth Survey of 47 Denominations in the United States and Canada with Interpretation by 18 Experts* (Harper & Row, 1980), pp. 60–68.

9. Neill Q. Hamilton, *Recovery of the Protestant Adventure* (Seabury Press, 1981).

10. Presbyterians are the most striking example of this conflict among denominations that attempt to practice "combined em-

phases." See Dean Hoge, *Division in the Protestant House: The Basic Reasons Behind Intra-Church Conflicts* (Westminster Press, 1976).

11. This term is Blizzard's, "The Parish Minister's Self-Image of His Master Role," *Pastoral Psychology,* Vol. 9, No. 89 (Dec. 1958), pp. 25–32.

12. Niebuhr, *The Purpose of the Church and Its Ministry,* p. 31.

13. Fowler, *Stages of Faith.*

14. Gail Sheehy, *Passages: Predictable Crises of Adult Life* (Bantam Books, 1976).

15. Daniel J. Levinson et al., *The Seasons of a Man's Life* (Alfred A. Knopf, 1978).

16. Albert C. Outler, ed., *John Wesley,* A Library of Protestant Thought (Oxford University Press, 1964), p. 251.

17. See Robert T. Handy, *A Christian America: Protestant Hopes and Historical Realities* (Oxford University Press, 1971), for the story of social perfectionism.

18. For this story, see Vinson Synan, *The Holiness-Pentecostal Movement in the United States* (Wm. B. Eerdmans Publishing Co., 1971).

19. See Richard Quebedeaux, *The New Charismatics: The Origins, Development, and Significance of Neo-Pentecostalism* (Doubleday & Co., 1976), for the story in America; Walter J. Hollenweger, *The Pentecostals: The Charismatic Movement in the Churches* (Augsburg Publishing House, 1972); and Arnold Bittlinger, ed., *The Church Is Charismatic: The World Council of Churches and the Charismatic Renewal* (Geneva: World Council of Churches, 1981), for the story worldwide.

20. The Greek words for an office simply do not occur in the New Testament. See Eduard Schweizer, *Church Order in the New Testament,* Studies in Biblical Theology, No. 32 (London: SCM Press, 1961), p. 171.

21. Otto Michel, "oikodomeō," in *Theologisches Wörterbuch zum Neuen Testament,* Vol. 5, ed. Gerhard Kittel (Stuttgart: W. Kohlhammer Verlag), pp. 142ff.

22. Joseph A. Fitzmyer, ed. and tr., *The Gospel According to Luke, I–IX,* The Anchor Bible, Vol. 28 (Doubleday & Co., 1981).

23. See Anselm Schulz, *Nachfolgen und Nachahmen* (Following and Imitating) (Munich: Kösel-Verlag, 1962), and Hans Dieter Betz, *Nachfolge und Nachahmung Jesu Christi im Neuen Testament* (Discipleship and Imitation of Jesus Christ in the New Testament) (Tübingen: J. C. B. Mohr [Paul Siebeck], 1967).

24. According to Conzelmann, Luke intended the time of Jesus' ministry to be a unique and unrepeatable "middle of time," the conditions of which could not have been continued into the time of the church. See Hans Conzelmann, *The Theology of St. Luke* (Harper & Brothers, 1960), pp. 170ff.

25. In the next chapter, I shall explain how it is especially appropriate to speak of the Spirit as feminine.

26. For an argument of this intention for Mark particularly, but for others as well, see Hamilton, *Recovery of the Protestant Adventure.*

27. Albert Schweitzer, *The Quest of the Historical Jesus* (London: Adam & Charles Black, 1952).

28. For the perspective of redaction criticism which this chapter assumes but which it is beyond the scope of this book to explain, see Norman Perrin, *What Is Redaction Criticism?* (Fortress Press, 1969), and Joachim Rohde, *Rediscovering the Teaching of the Evangelists,* The New Testament Library (Westminster Press, 1968).

29. Max Weber, *The Protestant Ethic and the Spirit of Capitalism* (Charles Scribner's Sons, 1958), p. 49.

30. For a detailed treatment of this pericope, see Hamilton, *Recovery of the Protestant Adventure,* pp. 108–113.

31. Joachim Jeremias, *The Prayers of Jesus* (Fortress Press, 1978), pp. 96ff.

32. See Janet F. Fishburn, *The Fatherhood of God and the Victorian Family: The Social Gospel in America* (Fortress Press, 1982). Some even suggest that women were treated more fairly in heretical sects: Elaine Pagels, *The Gnostic Gospels* (Random House, 1979), for which there is inadequate grounds; cf. Kathleen McVey, "Gnosticism, Feminism, and Elaine Pagels," *Theology Today,* Vol. 37, No. 4 (Jan. 1981), pp. 498–501.

33. Jürgen Moltmann's lecture, "A Doxological Concept of the Trinity," delivered at Moravian Theological Seminary, Bethlehem, Pa., Nov. 19, 1980.

34. Dennis J. Bennett, *Nine O'Clock in the Morning: An Episcopal Priest Discovers the Holy Spirit* (Logos International, 1970), pp. 106ff.

35. Russell H. Conwell, *Acres of Diamonds* (Harper & Brothers, 1915), p. 18. Taken from a prime example of the Gospel of Wealth, "Acres of Diamonds" was the most famous lecture of that time by a Baptist clergyman.

36. For a recent exposé of this last illusion, see Hamilton, *Recovery of the Protestant Adventure,* Pt. I.

37. See, for example, *Model for Ministry: A Report for Study Issued by the General Assembly Special Committee on the Theology of the Call,* Lewis Mudge, ed., with essays by Arthur C. Cochrane (Philadelphia: Office of the General Assembly of The United Presbyterian Church U.S.A., 1970).

38. Hoge, *Division in the Protestant House.*

39. Conway, *Men in Mid-Life Crisis,* Ch. 10, "The Affair," and Ch. 11, "Escaping the Affair."

40. In a footnote of the 1797 edition of his *Journal,* Wesley agreed with a Dr. Broughton who refused to believe that Wesley had not had faith before then. "He was in the right. I certainly then had the faith of a servant, though not of a son." (Outler, ed., *John Wesley,* p. 54, n. 2.)

41. Henry Scougal, *The Life of God in the Soul of Man,* arr. and ed. by Thomas S. Kepler for Living Selections from the Great Devotional Classics (Nashville: Upper Room, 1962), p. 10.

42. Professor Brown aptly makes the connection between John's picture of bestowing of the Spirit and Genesis, Wisdom, and Ezekiel without, however, coupling these to the situation of John. (Raymond E. Brown, *The Gospel According to John, XIII–XXI,* The Anchor Bible, Vol. 29A, pp. 1037ff.; Doubleday & Co., 1970.)

43. Charles H. Dodd, *The Interpretation of the Fourth Gospel* (Cambridge University Press, 1953), p. 414.

44. William F. Arndt and F. Wilbur Gingrich, *A Greek-English Lexicon of the New Testament and Other Early Christian Literature,* being a translation and adaptation of Walter Bauer's original work (University of Chicago Press, 1957), p. 623.

45. Ernst Haenchen, *The Acts of the Apostles: A Commentary* (Westminster Press, 1971), p. 171, n. 2.

46. Against Haenchen, who declares that ecstatic speech is meant but provides no argument. After the pattern set by Isaiah, Jesus, Joel, and Pentecost, the burden of proof is on anyone who claims that Luke means anything other than foreign languages.

47. John Koenig calls this "the confidence of faith" in *Charismata: God's Gifts for God's People* (Westminster Press, 1978), p. 53. No other single book I know describes so thoroughly the multifaceted experience of the Holy Spirit in the New Testament that I am calling transition into life in the Spirit. I am indebted to it for stimulation even where I do not cite it specifically. I would make it required reading for any who wish to broaden their understanding of a subject I am only able to introduce within the scope of this chapter.

48. Perhaps the Quakers as a denomination understand this life of prayer better than any others do since they are organized around the recognition of the divine presence within making them in effect a community that grounds itself in transition into life in the Spirit.

49. For most of this section I am indebted to the stimulation of Professor Moltmann to be found in *The Trinity and the Kingdom* (Harper & Row, 1981), pp. 151–188, and in the lecture "A Doxological Concept of the Trinity," delivered at Moravian Theological Seminary in Bethlehem, Pa., in 1980 expanding this theme of the book. This remark on monotheism and pantheism is found in the book at p. 165, as well as in the lecture.

50. Moltmann, *The Trinity and the Kingdom*, p. 165.

51. The companion metaphor is to "walk by the Spirit," emphasizing the comprehensive scope of the Spirit's leading (Gal. 5:16, 25; Rom. 6:4; 8:4; cf. Eph. 5:2, 8; I John 1:7).

52. Thomas R. Kelly, *Testament of Devotion* (Harper & Brothers, 1941), p. 124.

53. Brother Lawrence, *The Practice of the Presence of God*, arr. and ed. by Douglas V. Steere for Living Selections from the Great Devotional Classics (Nashville: Upper Room, 1950).

54. This vulnerability is reflected in the pericope threatening dire consequences to those who cause "little ones," i.e., new converts, to stumble (Mark 9:42–50 and pars.).

55. Outler, *John Wesley*, p. 69.

56. Schweizer, *Church Order in the New Testament*, pp. 94ff.

57. Other occurrences of "charisma" are sexual continence (I Cor. 7:7) and office (I Tim. 4:14; II Tim. 1:6) when the Pauline idea of church as body has faded.

58. "He [Paul] includes among the gifts of grace the performance of such 'natural' ministries as the guidance of the Church, or the care of other people—things that it would never have entered the Corinthians' heads to regard as the effects of the Spirit." (Schweizer, *Church Order in the New Testament*, p. 102.)

59. Kelly, *A Testament of Devotion*, pp. 123, 100.

60. Eduard Schweizer, *Neotestamentica* (Zurich: Zwingli Verlag, 1963), p. 290.

61. Schweizer, "The Church as the Missionary Body of Christ," in *Neotestamentica*, pp. 312–329.

62. John G. Gager, *Kingdom and Community: The Social World of Early Christianity* (Prentice-Hall, 1975), p. 131.

63. Ibid., pp. 130f.

64. J. Christiaan Beker, *Paul the Apostle: The Triumph of God in Life and Thought* (Fortress Press, 1980), pp. 363ff.

65. "Through the mercies of the Almighty, I had, in a good degree, learned to be content with a plain way of living. I had but a small family. . . . Then I lessened my outward business, and, as I had opportunity, told my customers of my intentions, that they might consider what shop to turn to; and in a while I wholly laid down merchandise and followed my trade as a tailor by myself, having no apprentice. I also had a nursery of apple trees." (*The Journal of John Woolman*, ed. with an intro. by Thomas S. Kepler, pp. 43–44; World Publishing Co., 1954.) Woolman's remaining two occupations gave him most freedom to follow his "concern" which included Indians with whom he visited and his countrymen in England where he died of smallpox while pursuing his concern there.

66. *Theological Wordbook of the New Testament,* Vol. 4, p. 591.

67. The Division of Ordained Ministry of The United Methodist Church is sponsoring a Task Force on Spiritual Formation Among Methodist-related Seminaries; the Association of Theological Schools is sponsoring a project on spiritual formation.

68. James Fowler's work does not help in the specific way clergy need it most. The notion of maturing he describes is religious maturing in general, regardless of specific religious convictions. No doubt this will be helpful for purposes of interfaith dialogue or in interfaith settings such as public education where particular religious allegiances must remain muted. But the pastoral leader is responsible to a confessing community committed to Christian maturing in particular. Only the notion of specifically Christian maturing and the special means appropriate to that end are finally of use to ministers as prophetic guides to maturing in the Christian life, since it is part of the confessing consciousness of the churches they lead that Christian faith and life are not the same as in any other religion.

69. Levinson et al., *The Seasons of a Man's Life;* Sheehy, *Passages: Predictable Crises of Adult Life.*

70. St. Francis de Sales, *Introduction to the Devout Life,* tr. with an Intro. and Notes by John K. Ryan (Image Books, 1972), p. 37.

71. Neill Q. Hamilton, "Temple Cleansing and Temple Bank," *Journal of Biblical Theology,* Vol. 83 (1964), pp. 365ff.

72. Gager, *Kingdom and Community,* p. 130.